This book belongs to

- -

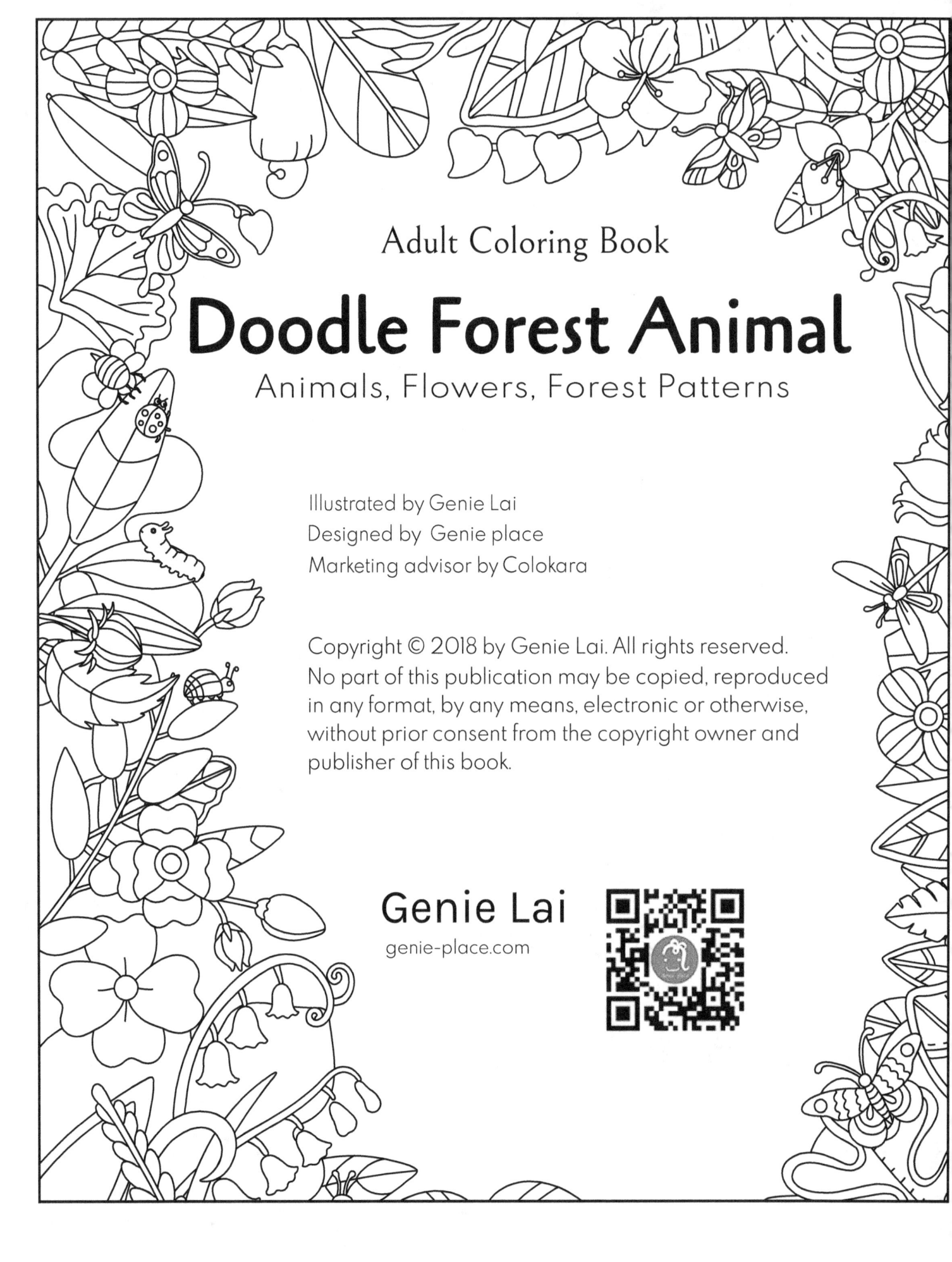

Adult Coloring Book

Doodle Forest Animal

Animals, Flowers, Forest Patterns

Illustrated by Genie Lai
Designed by Genie place
Marketing advisor by Colokara

Genie Lai
genie-place.com

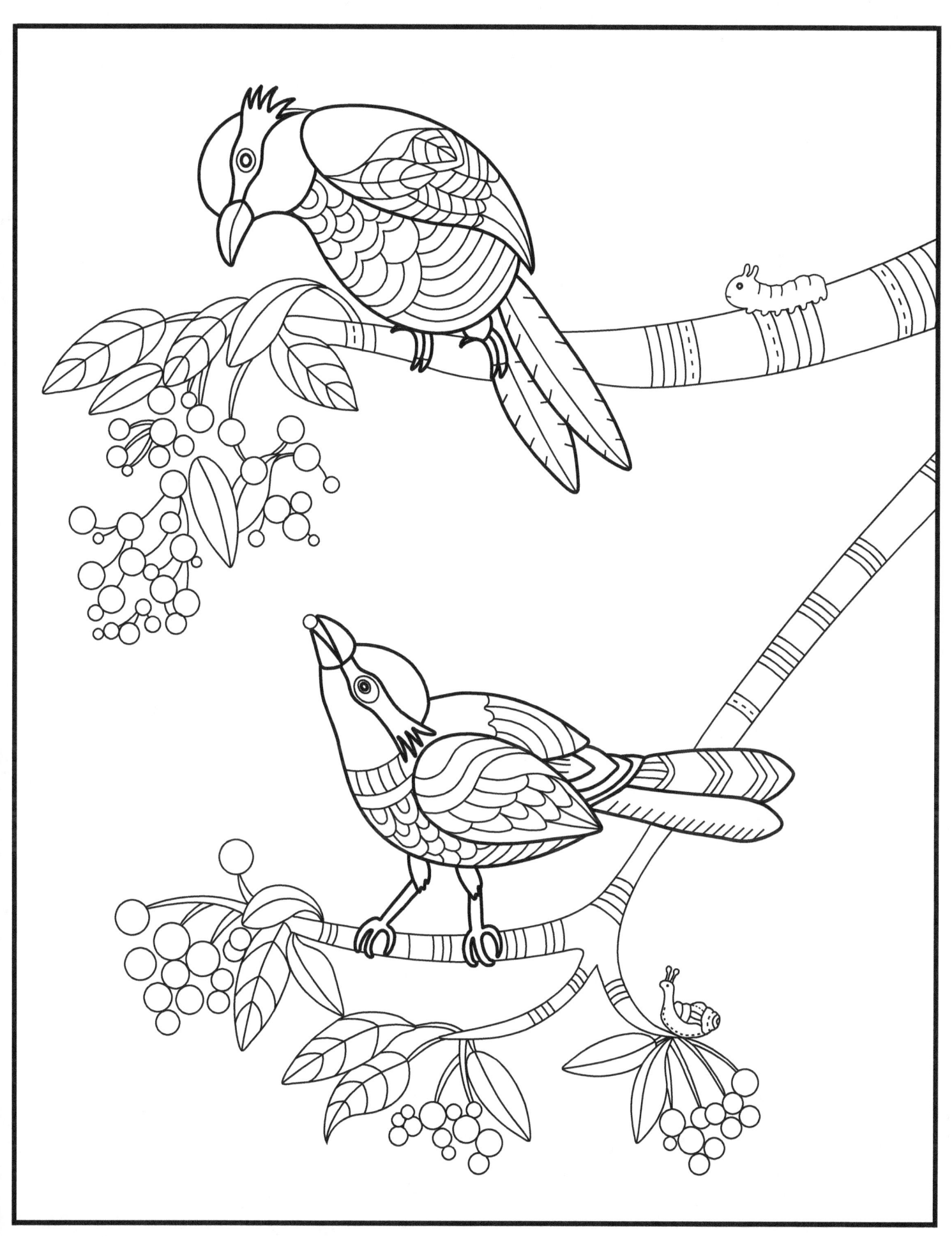

White-eared Sibia (*Heterophasia auricularis*).

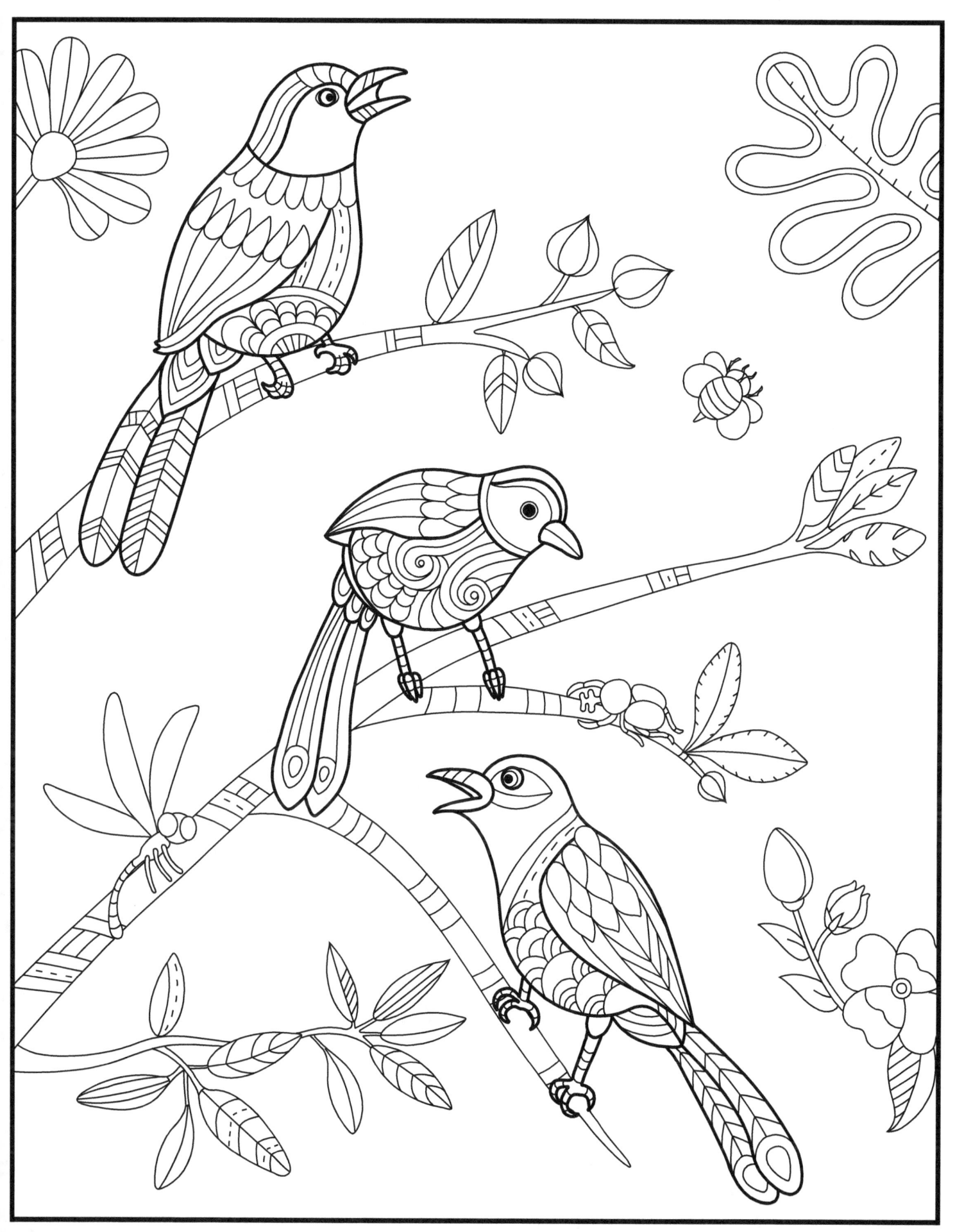

Taiwan Hwamei (*Garrulax taewanus*).

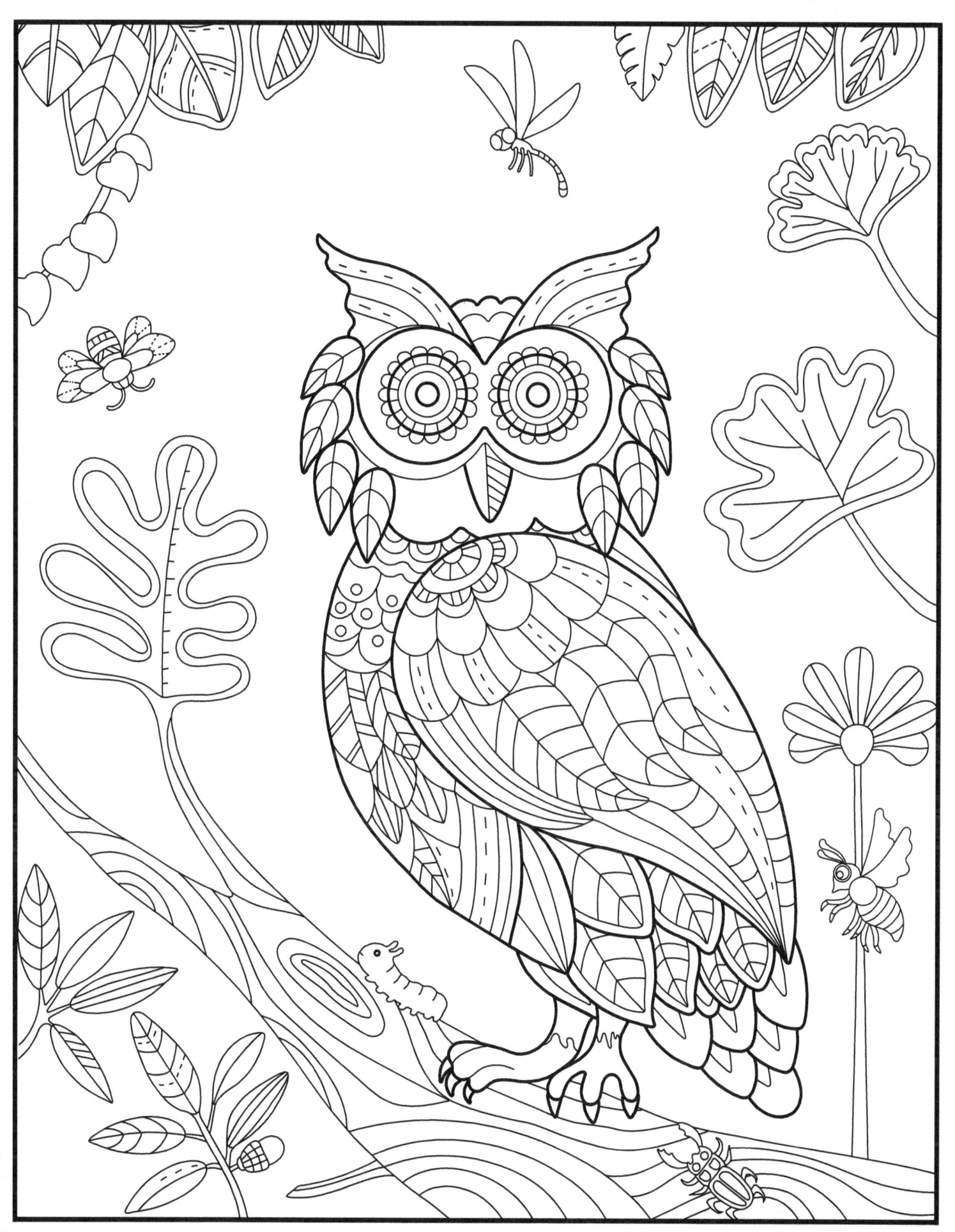

Lanyu Scops Owl (*Otus elegans*).

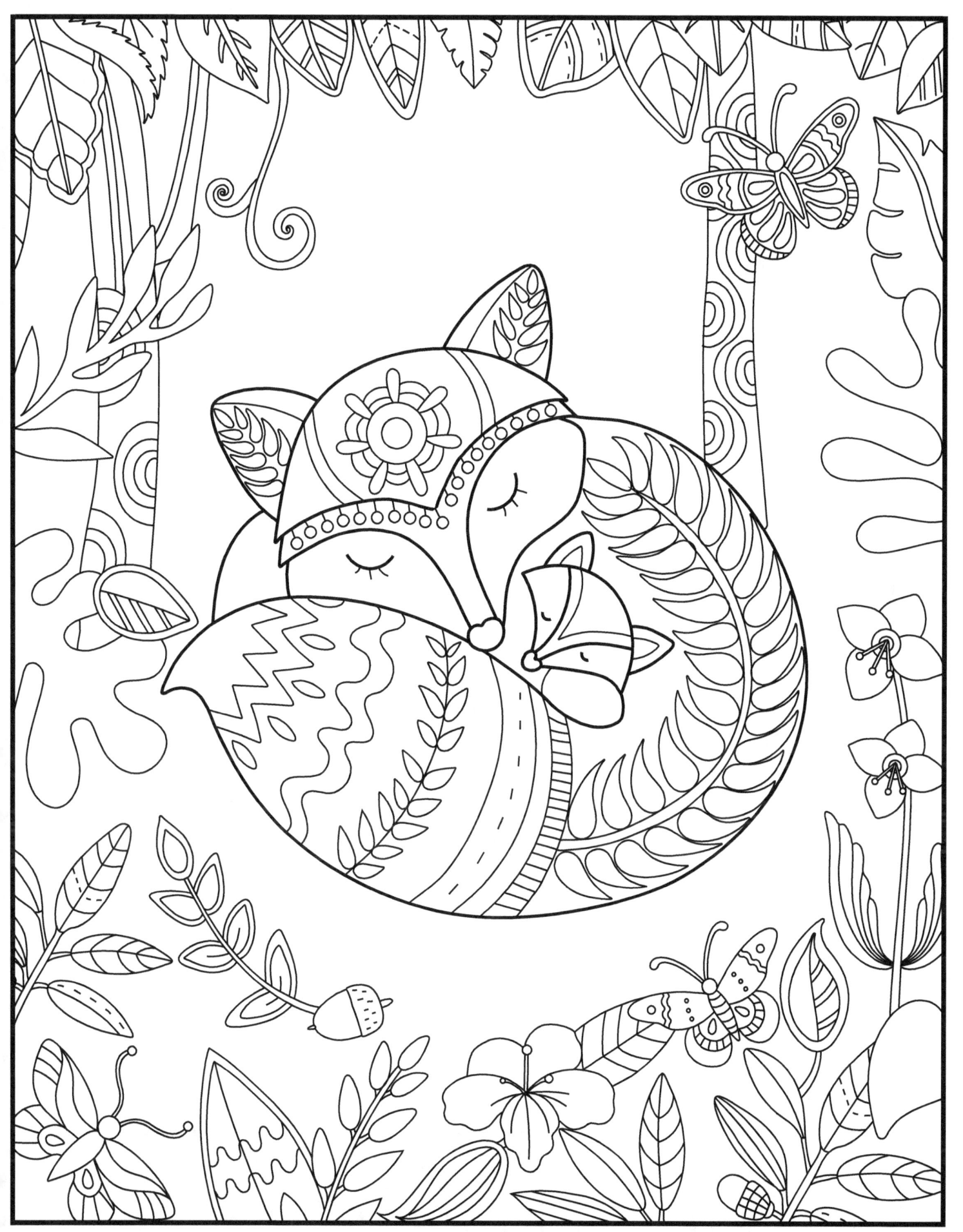

Red Fox (*Vulpes vulpes*).

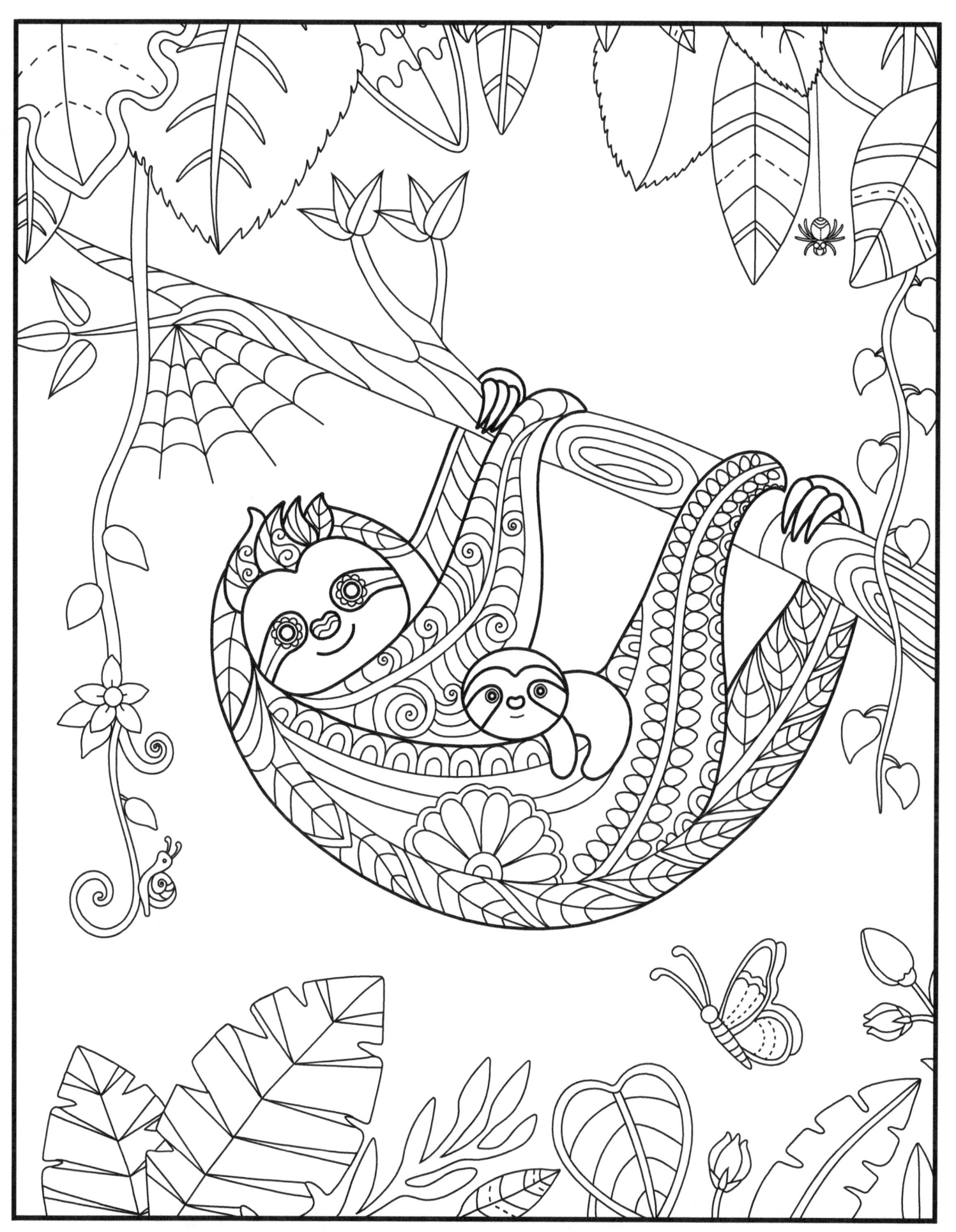

Pale-throated three-toed sloth (*Bradypus tridactylus*).

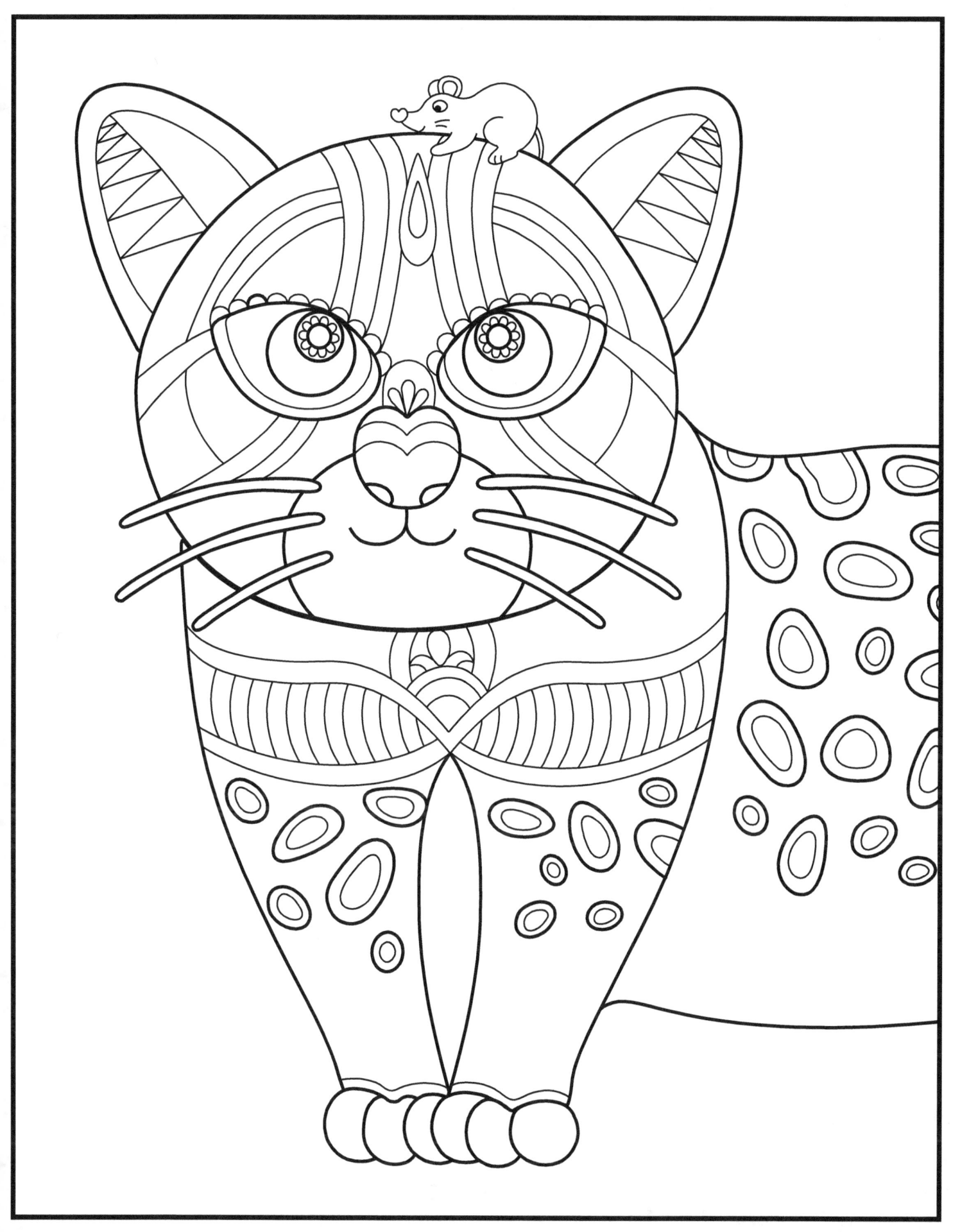

Leopard Cat (*Prionailurus bengalensis*).

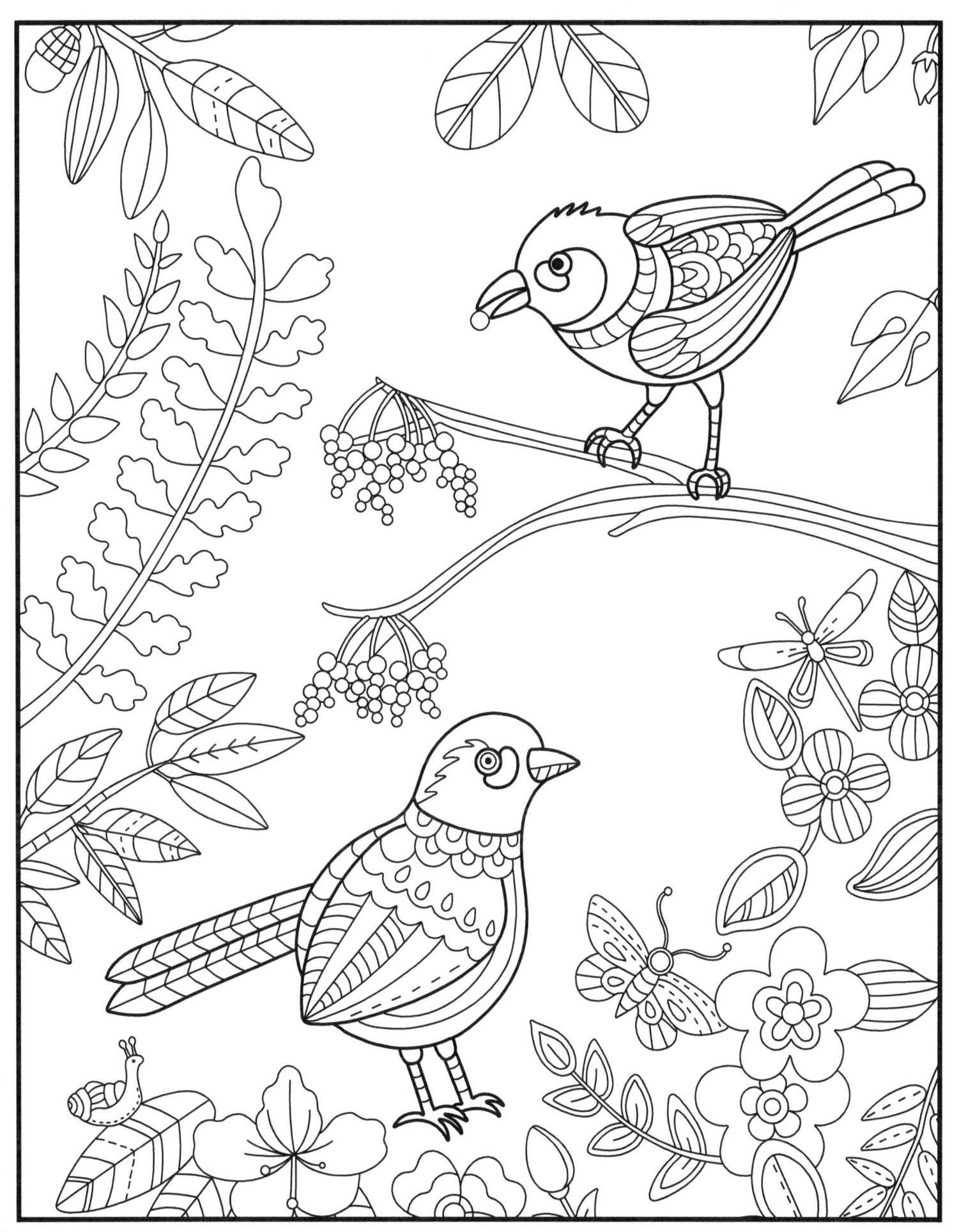

Steere's Liocichla (*Liocichla steerii*).

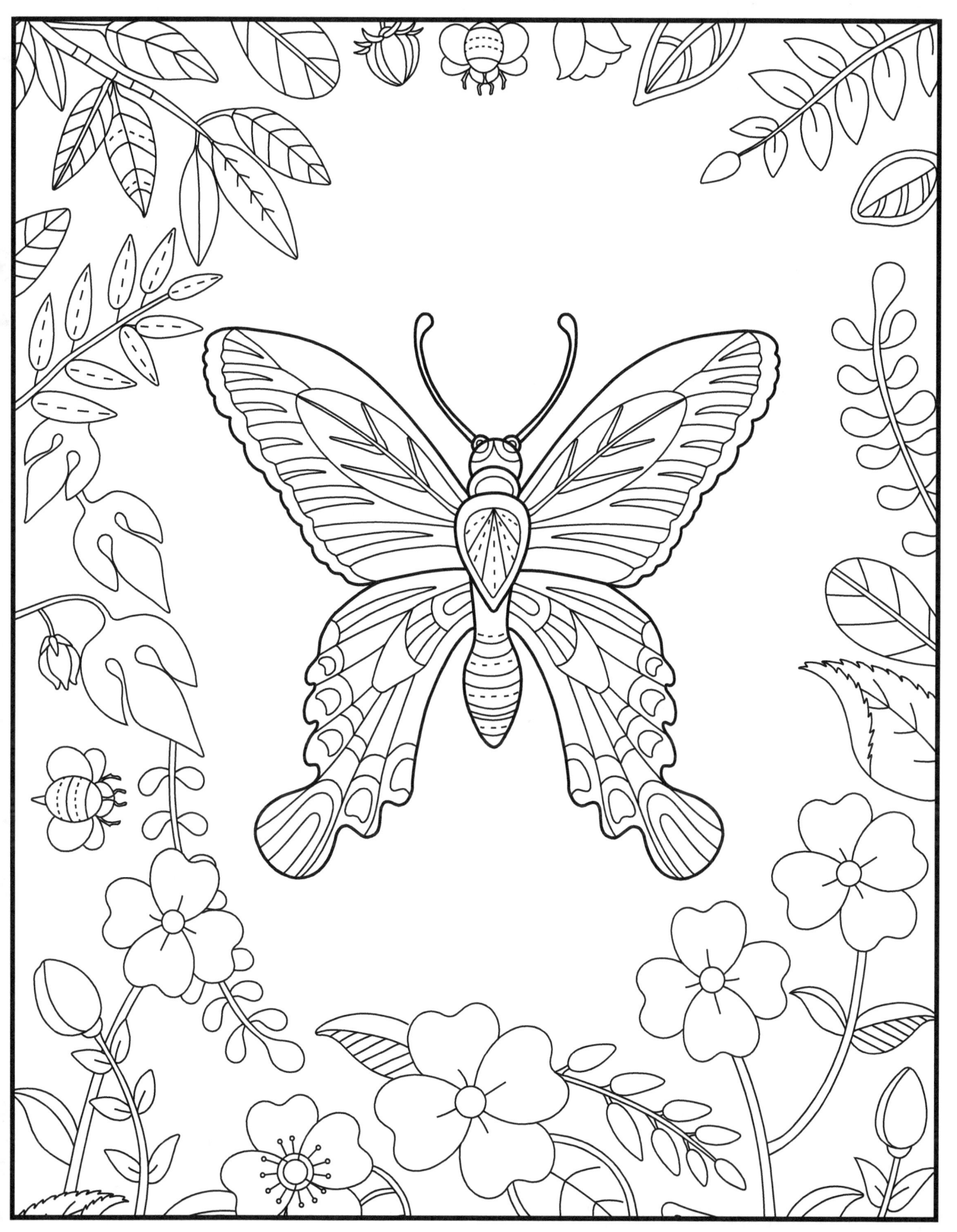

Broad-tailed Swallowtail Butterfly (*Agehana maraho*).

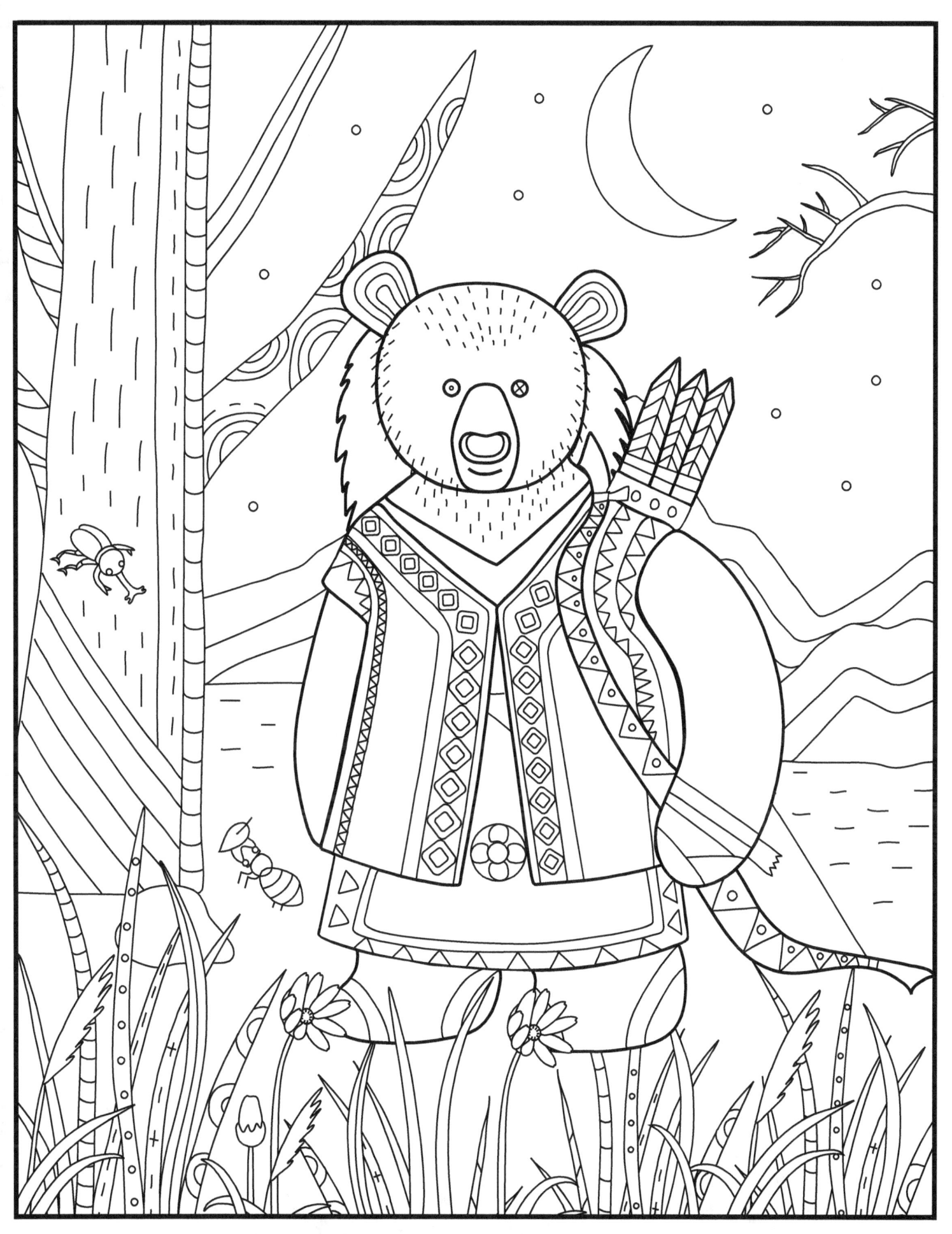

Formosan Black Bear (*Ursus thibetanus formosanus*).

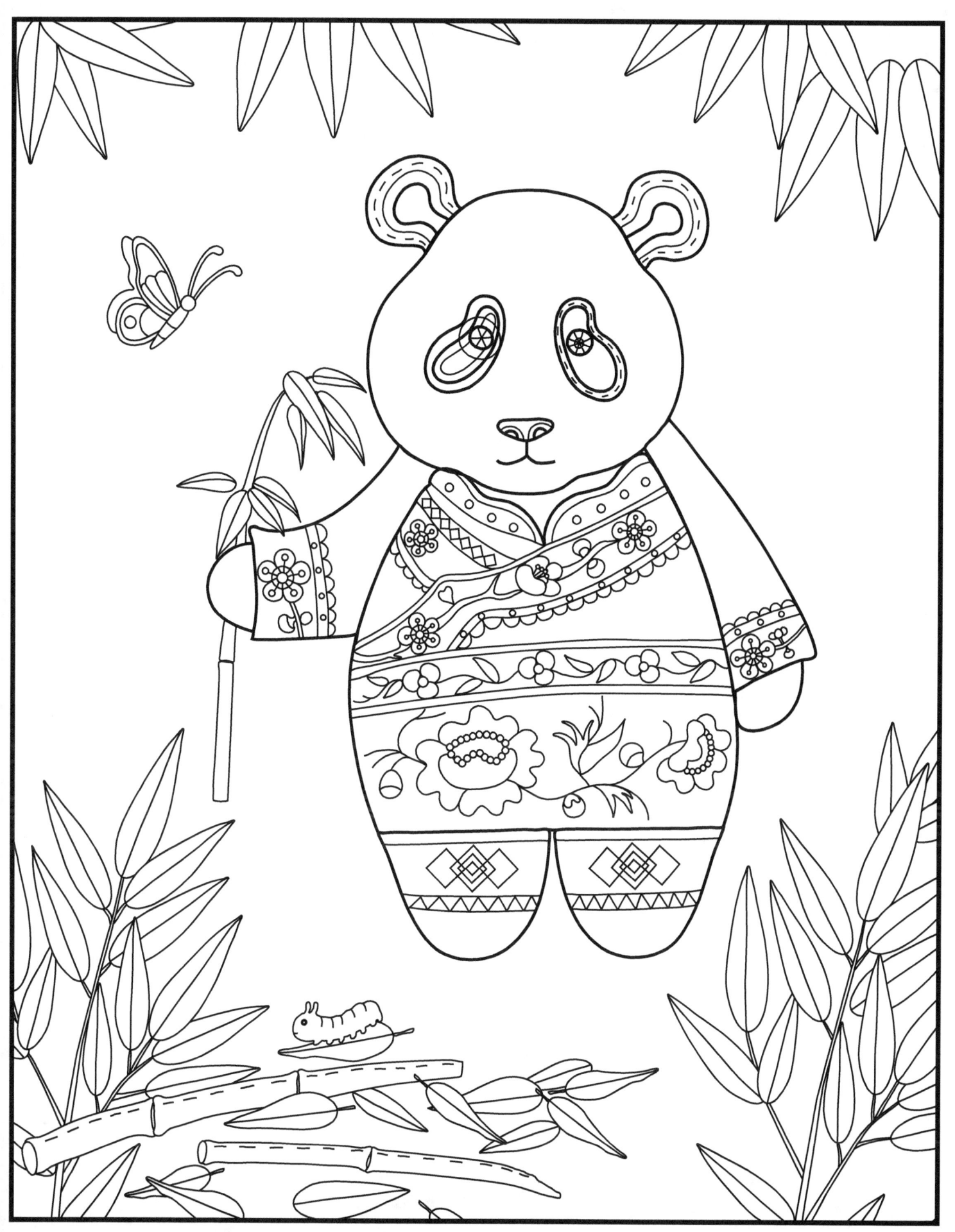

Giant Panda (*Ailuropoda melanoleuca*).

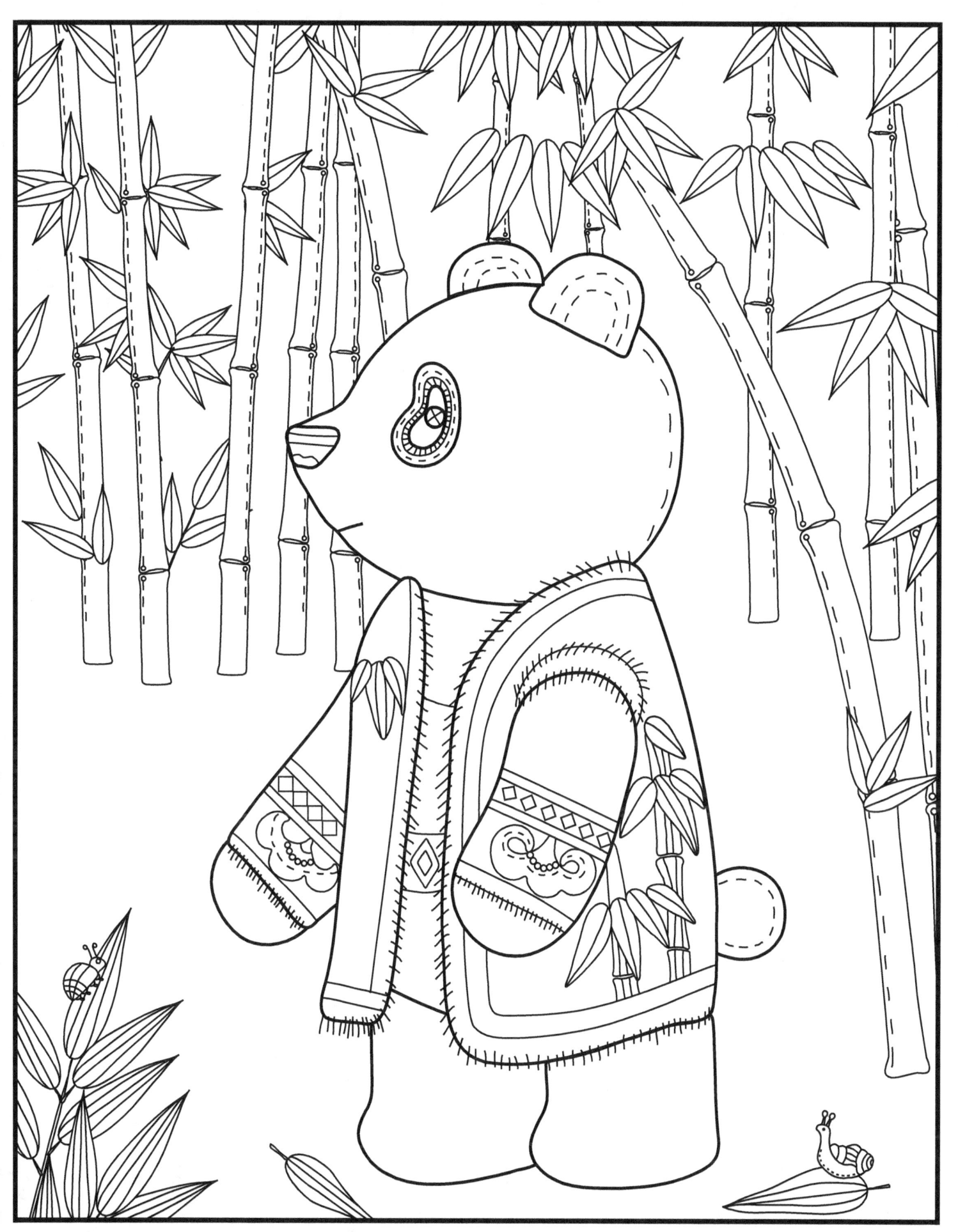

Giant Panda (*Ailuropoda melanoleuca*).

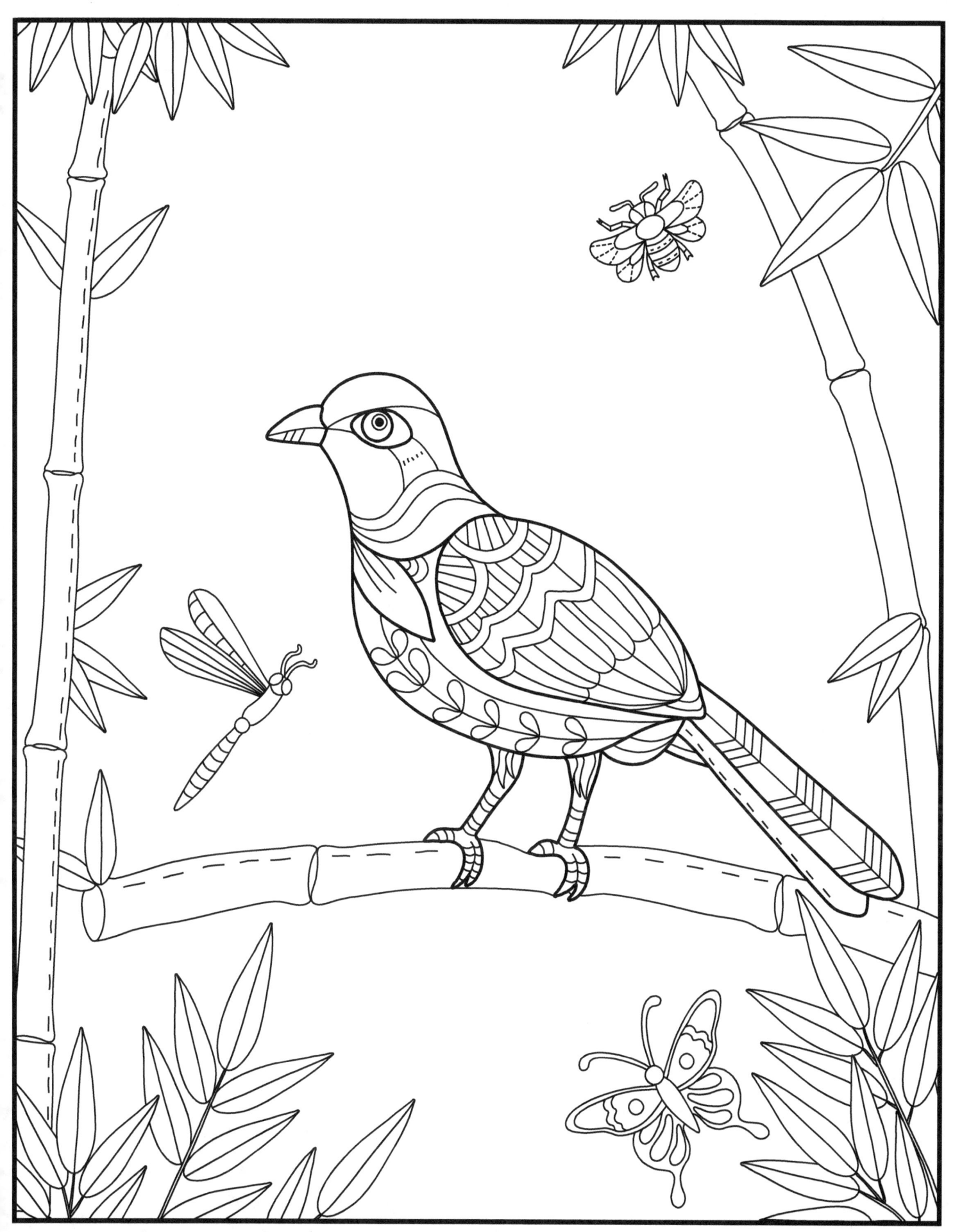

Rusty Laughingthrush (*Garrulax poecilorhynchus*).

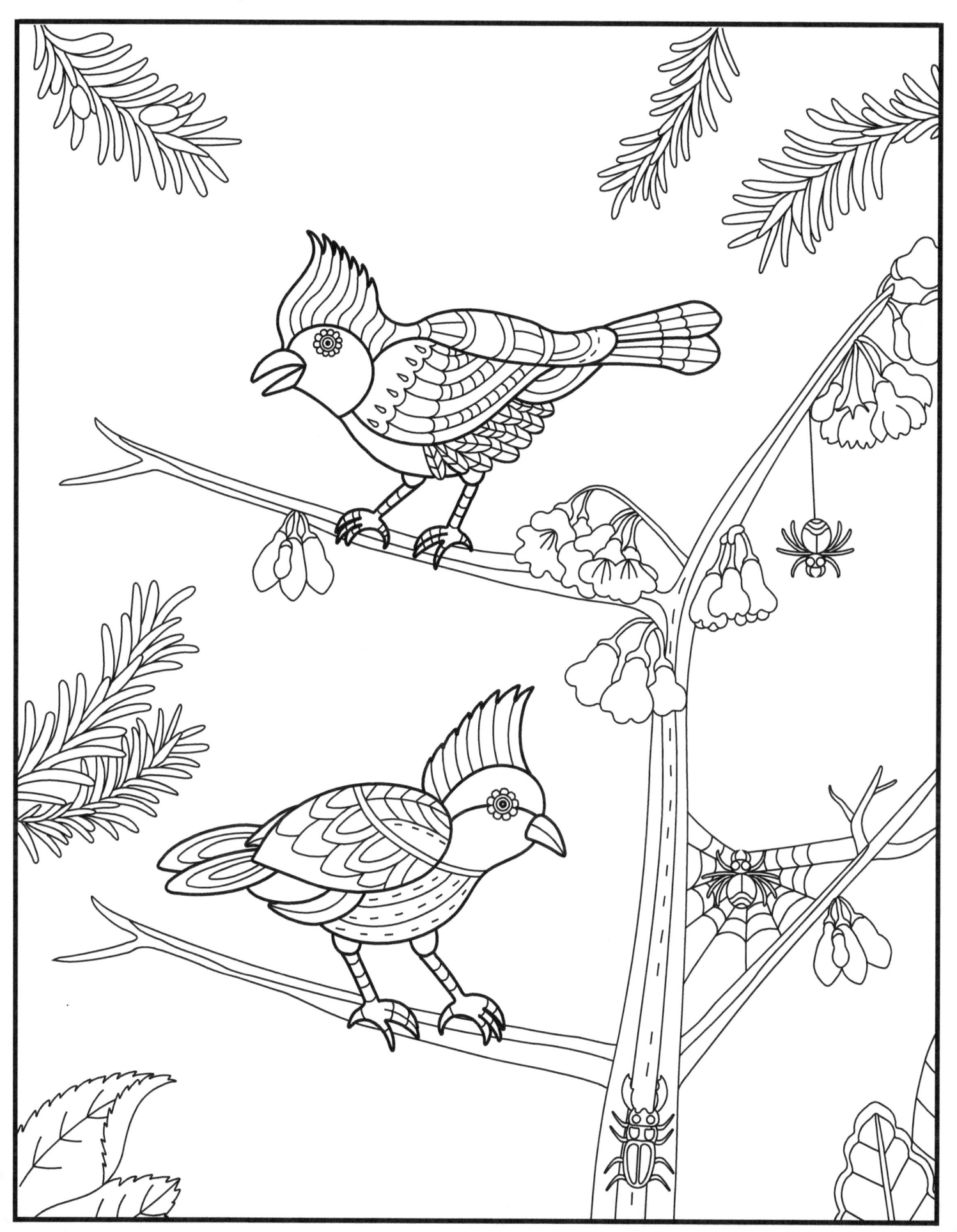

Taiwan Yuhina (*Yuhina brunneiceps*).

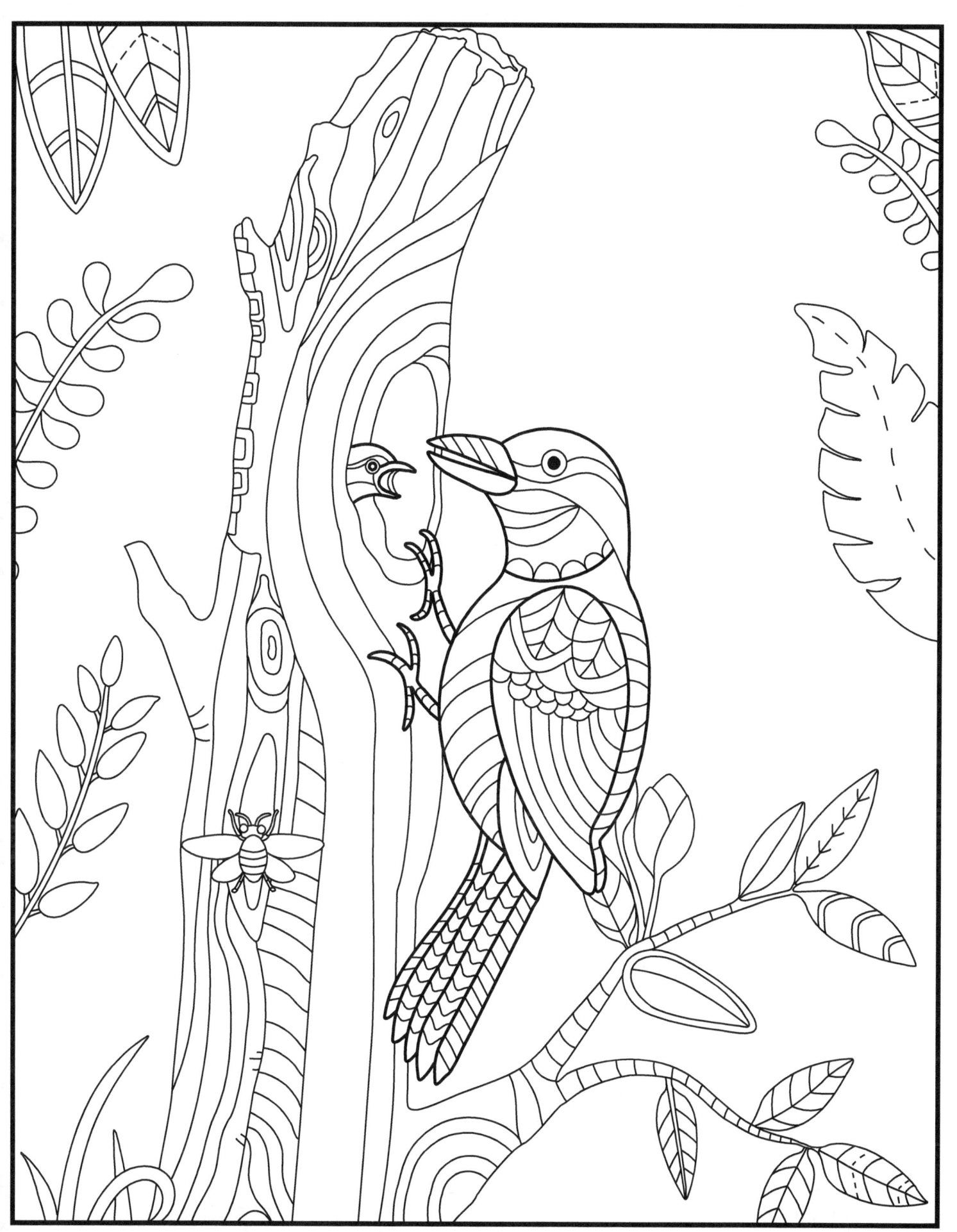

Taiwan Barbet (*Psilopogon nuchalis*).

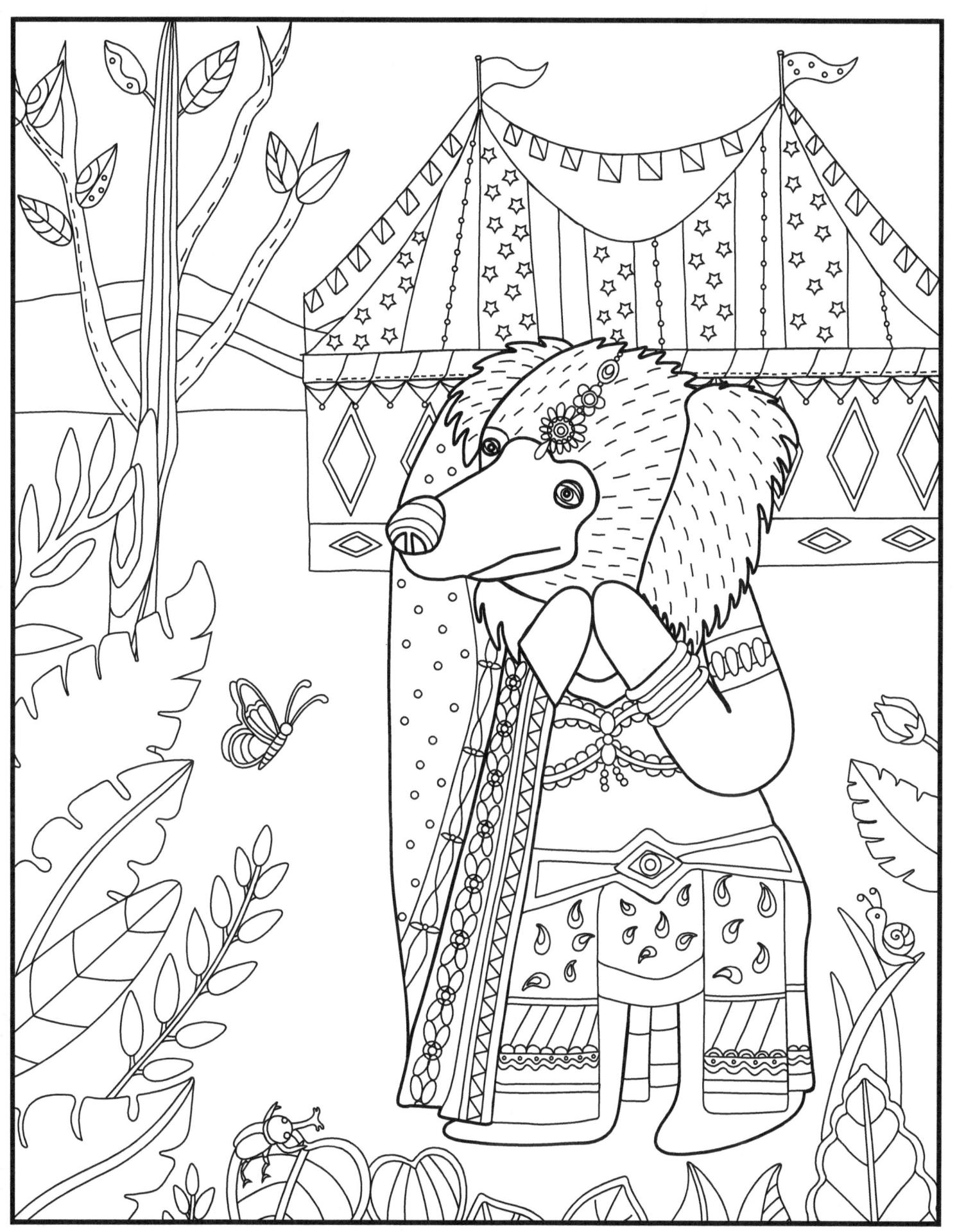

Sloth bear (*Melursus ursinus*).

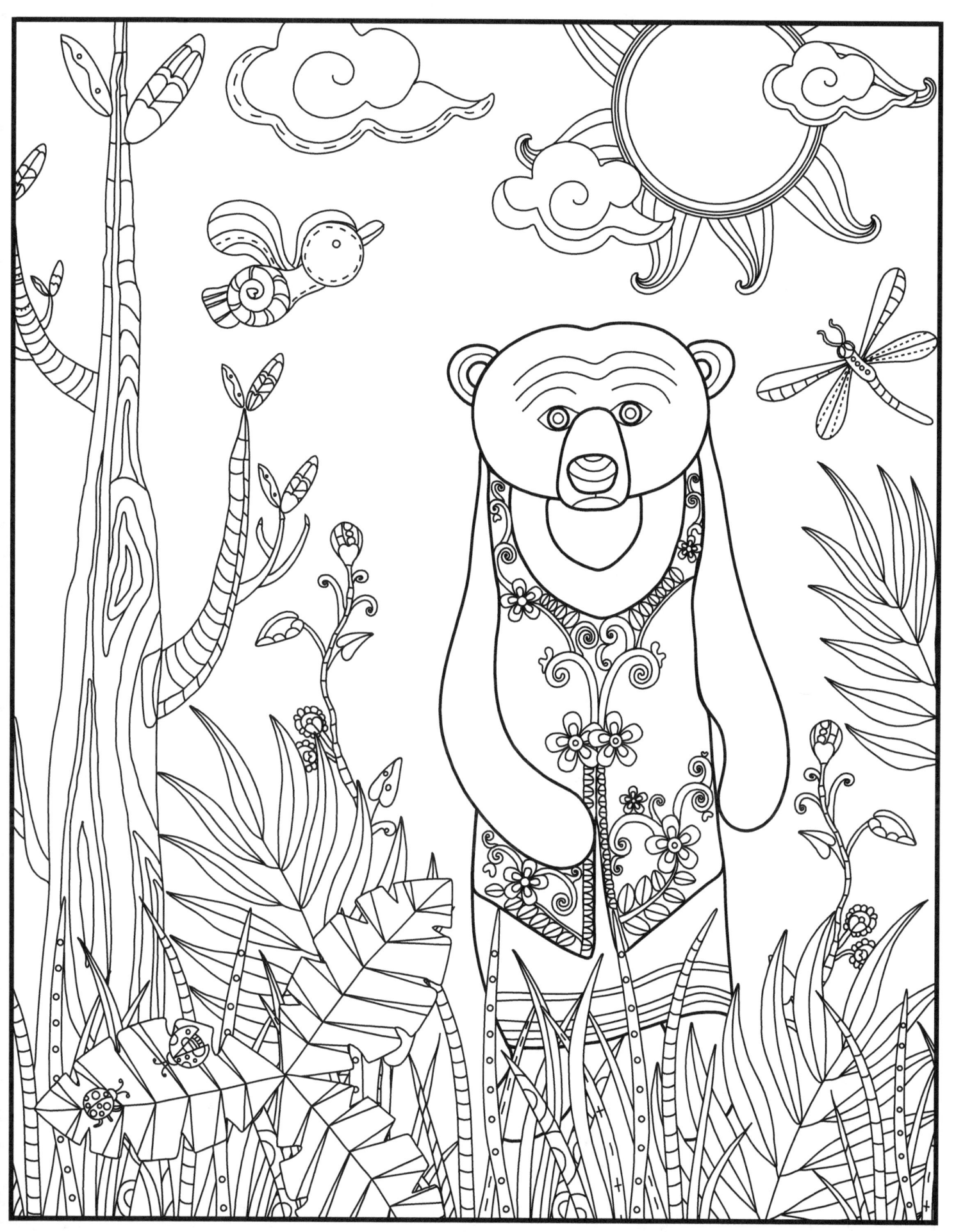

Sun bear (*Helarctos malayanus*).

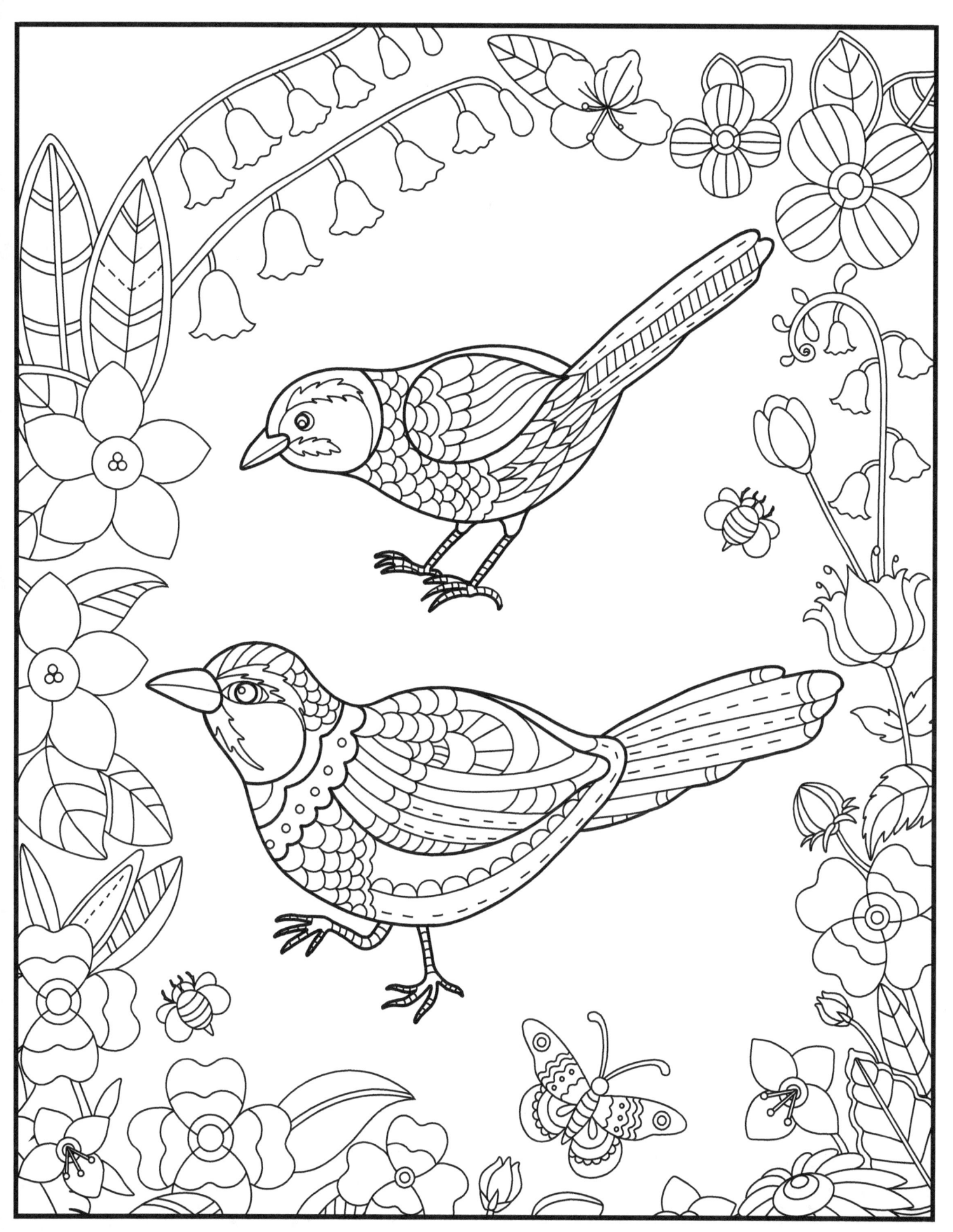

White-whiskered Laughingthrush (*Garrulax morrisonianus*).

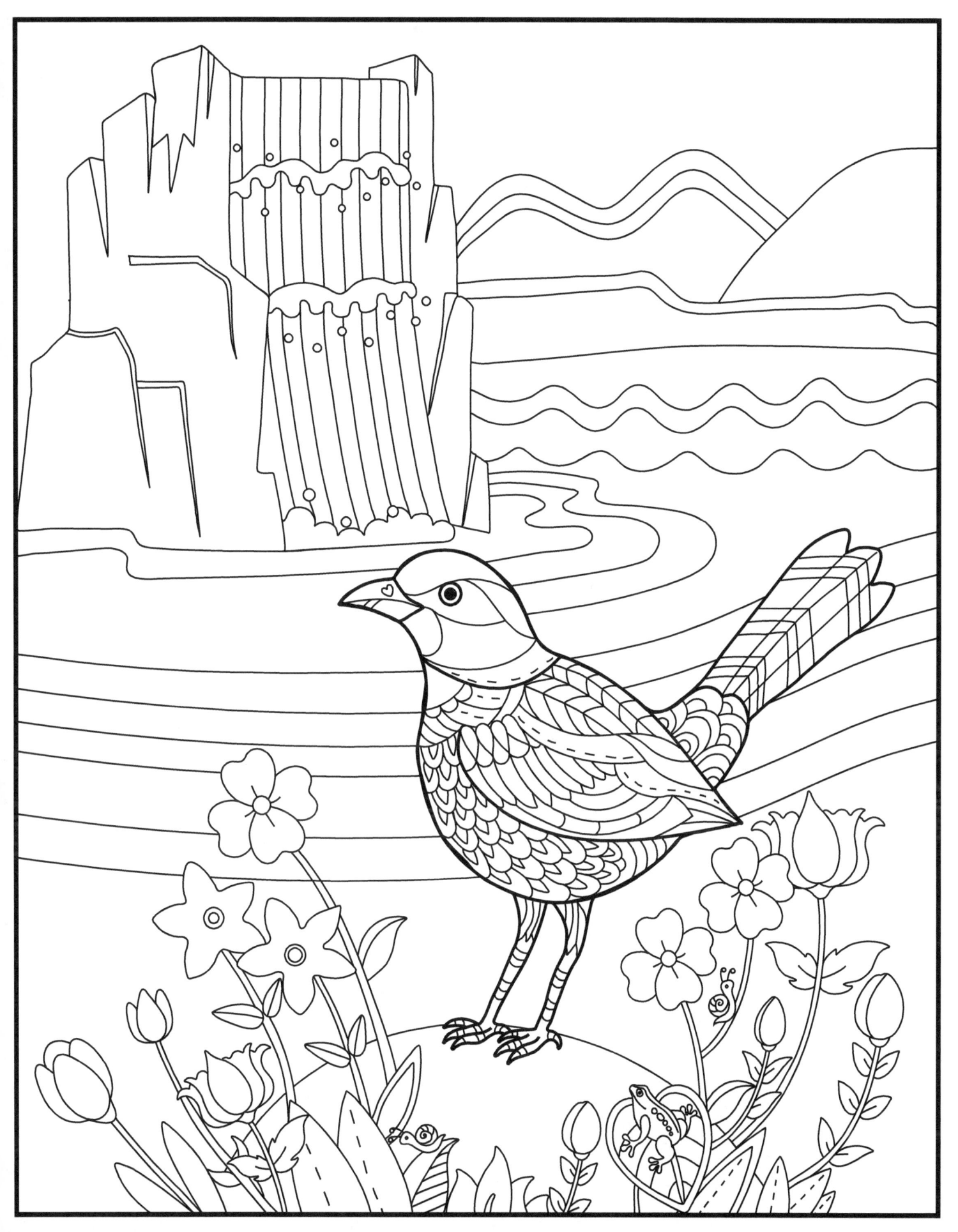

Taiwan Whistling-Thrush (*Myophonus insularis*).

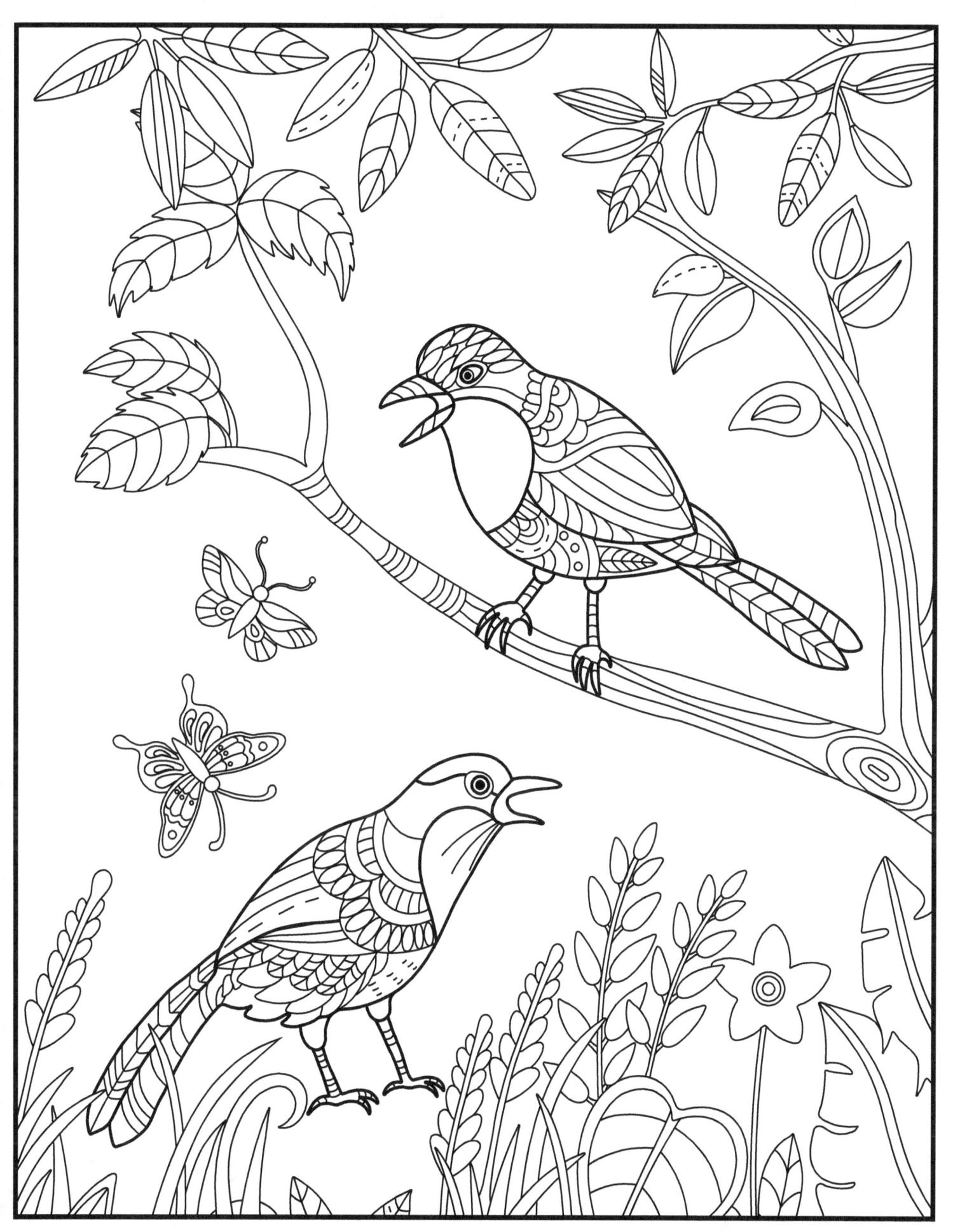

Rufous-crowned Laughingthrush (*Pterorhinus ruficeps*).

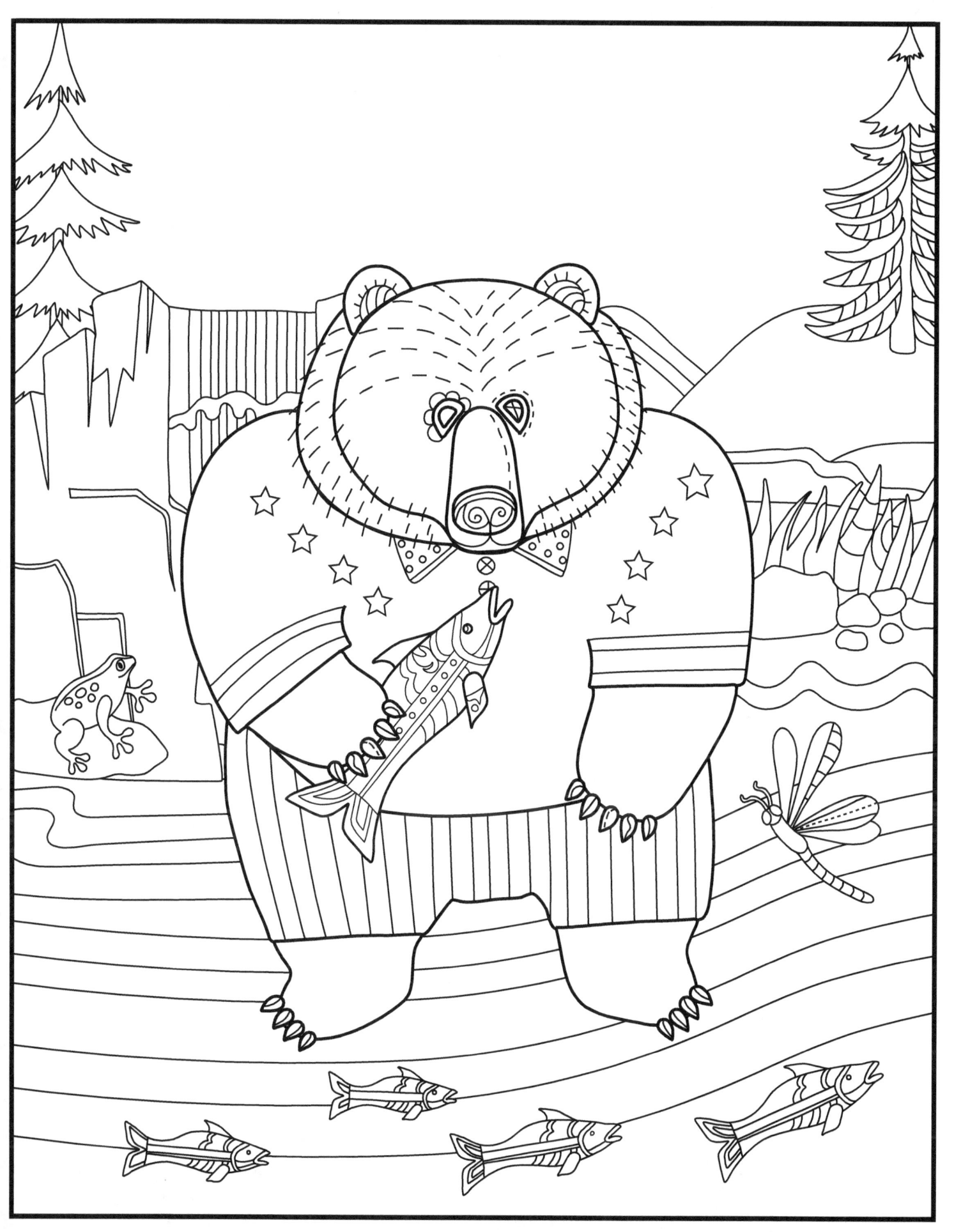

Brown Bear (*Ursus arctos*).

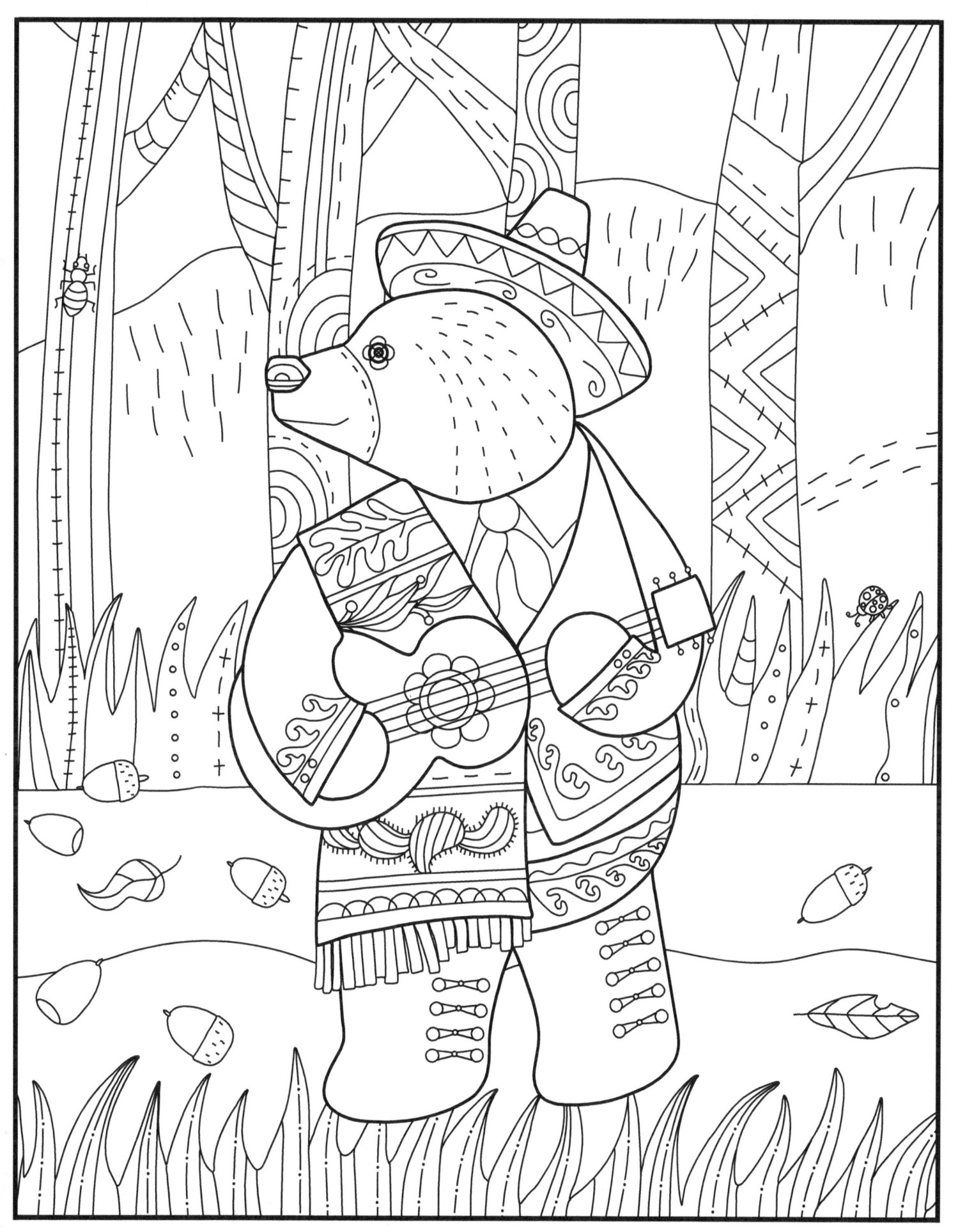

American black bear (*Ursus americanus*).

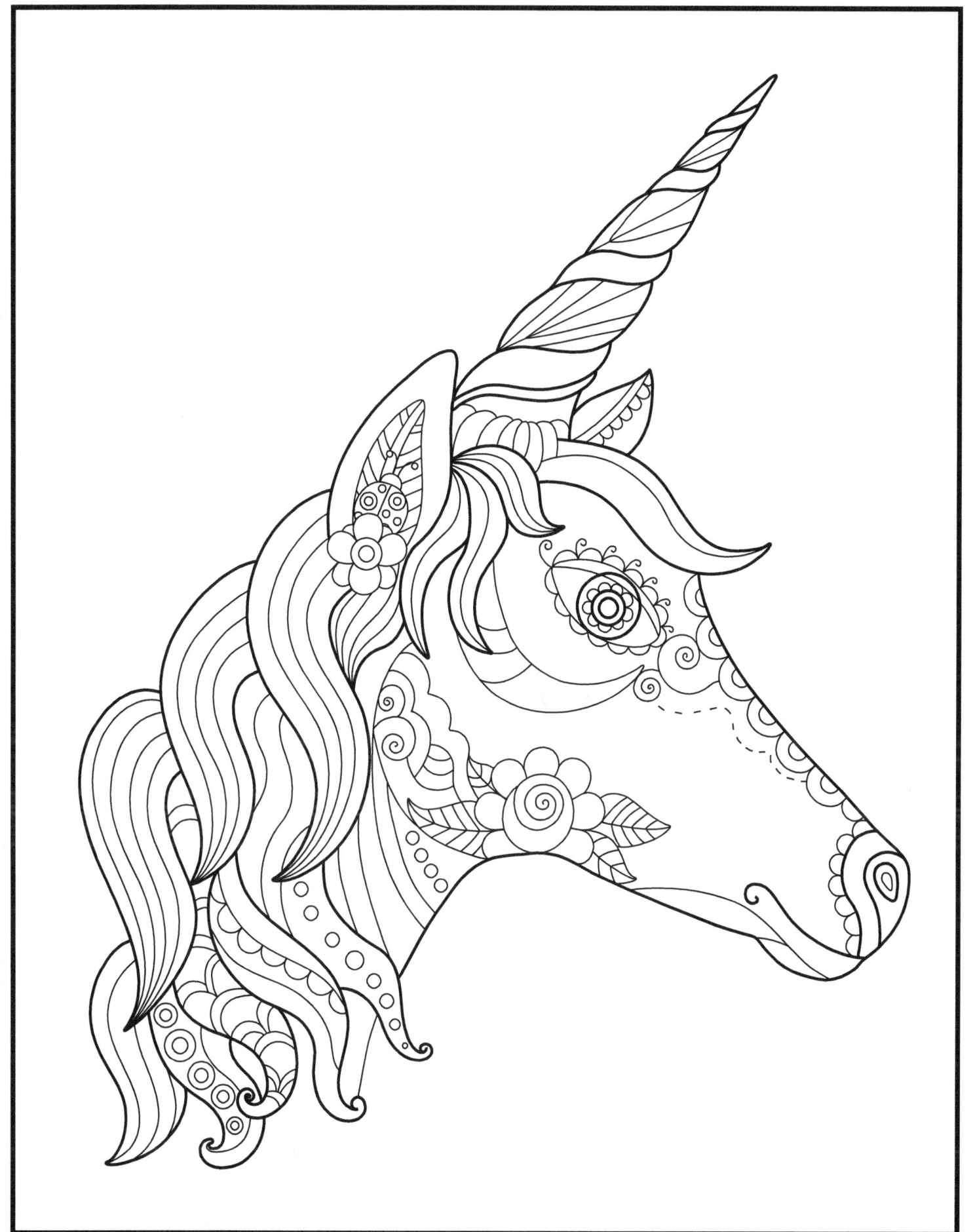

Unicorn

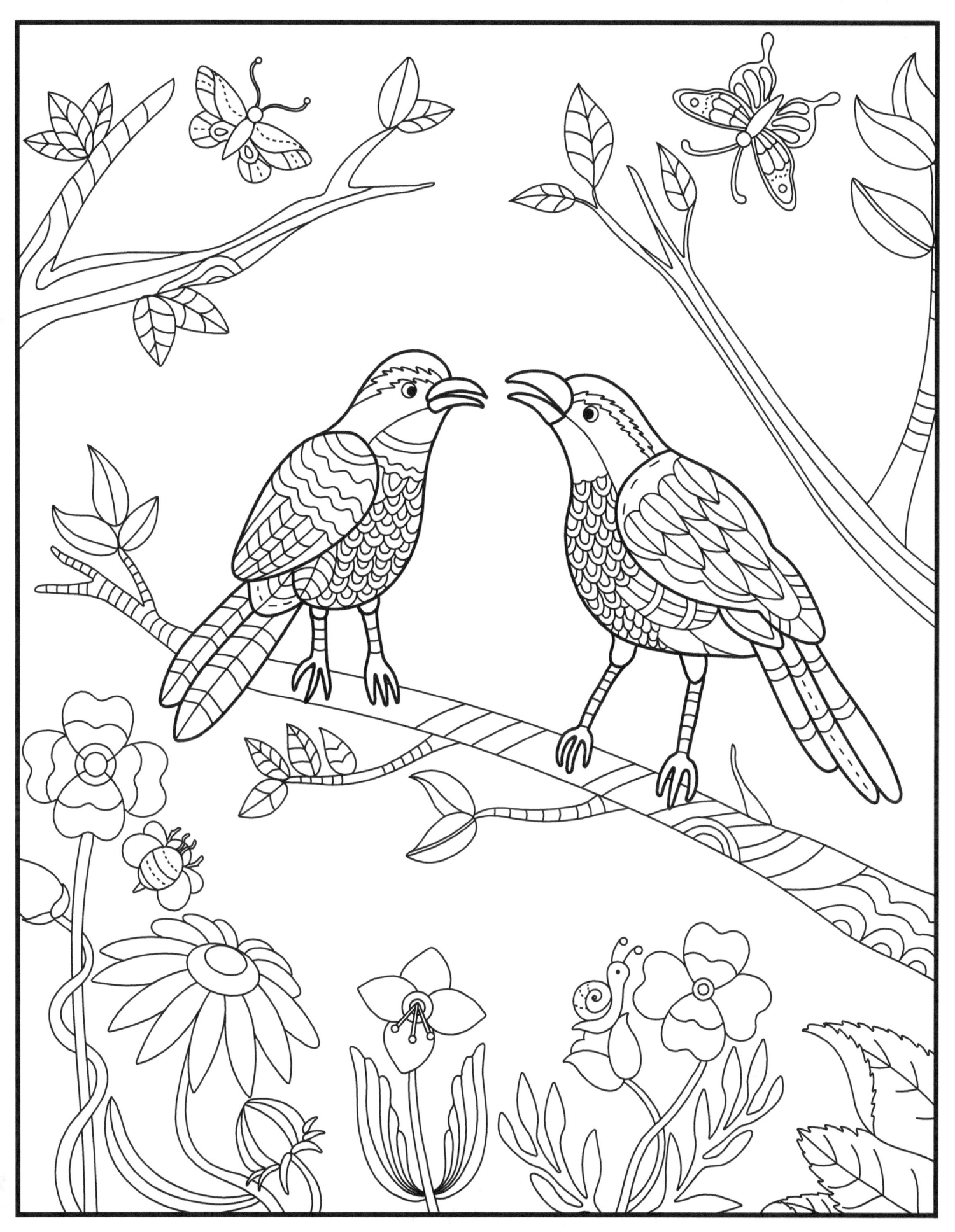

Taiwan Scimitar-babbler (*Pomatorhinus musicus*).

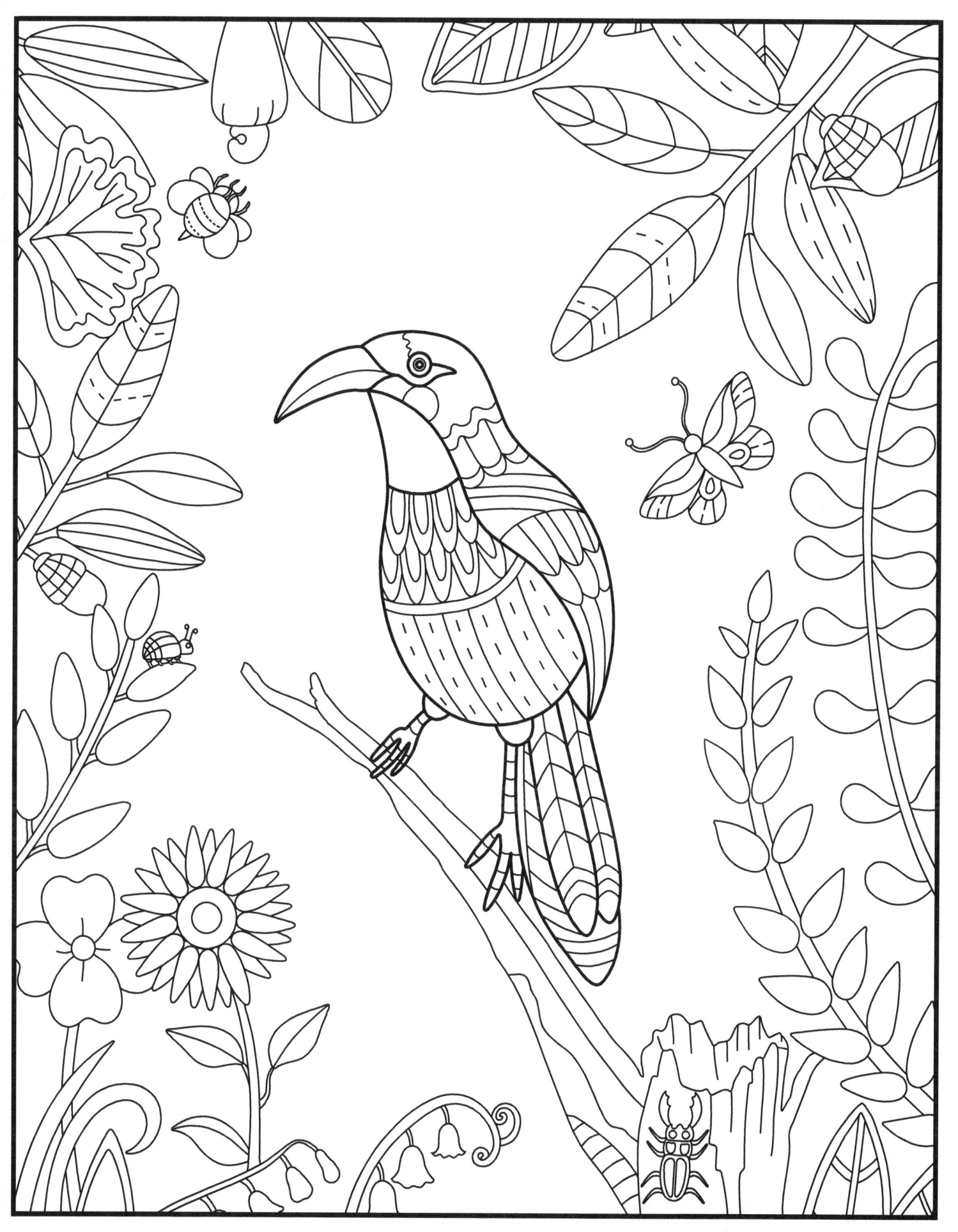

Rusty-cheeked Scimitar Babbler (*Pomatorhinus erythrogenys*).

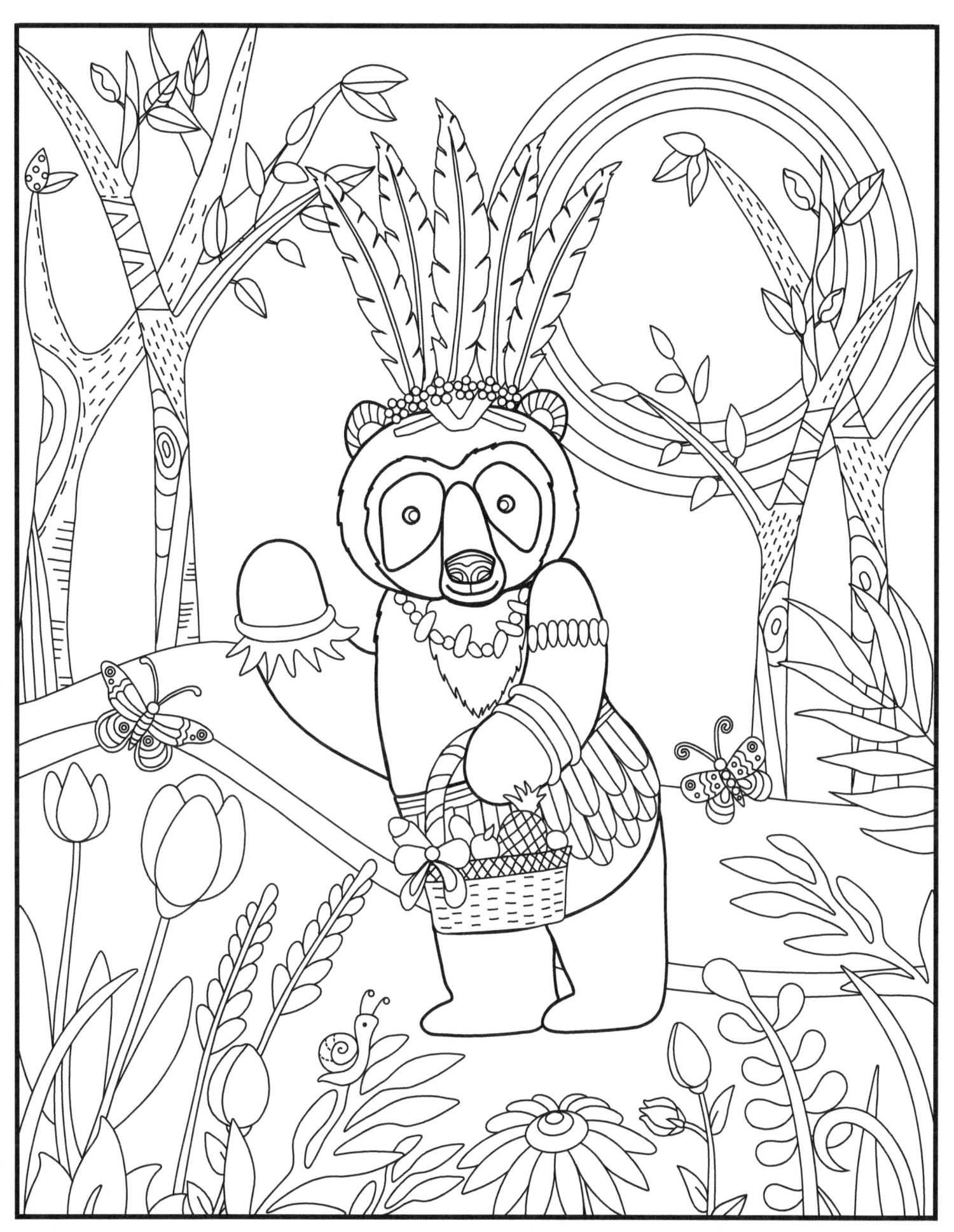

Spectacle Bear (*Tremarctos ornatus*).

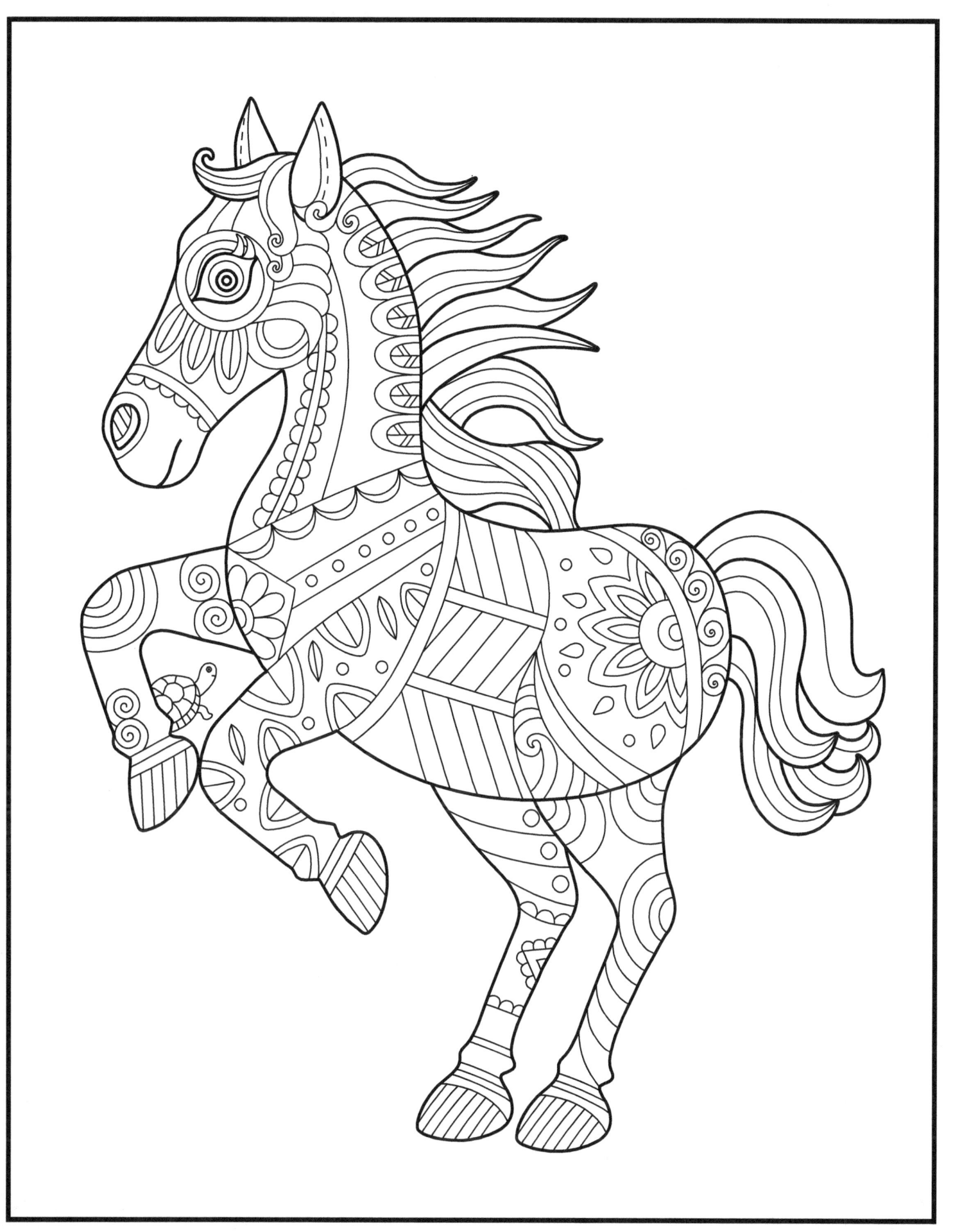

American Quarter Horse (*Equus caballus*).

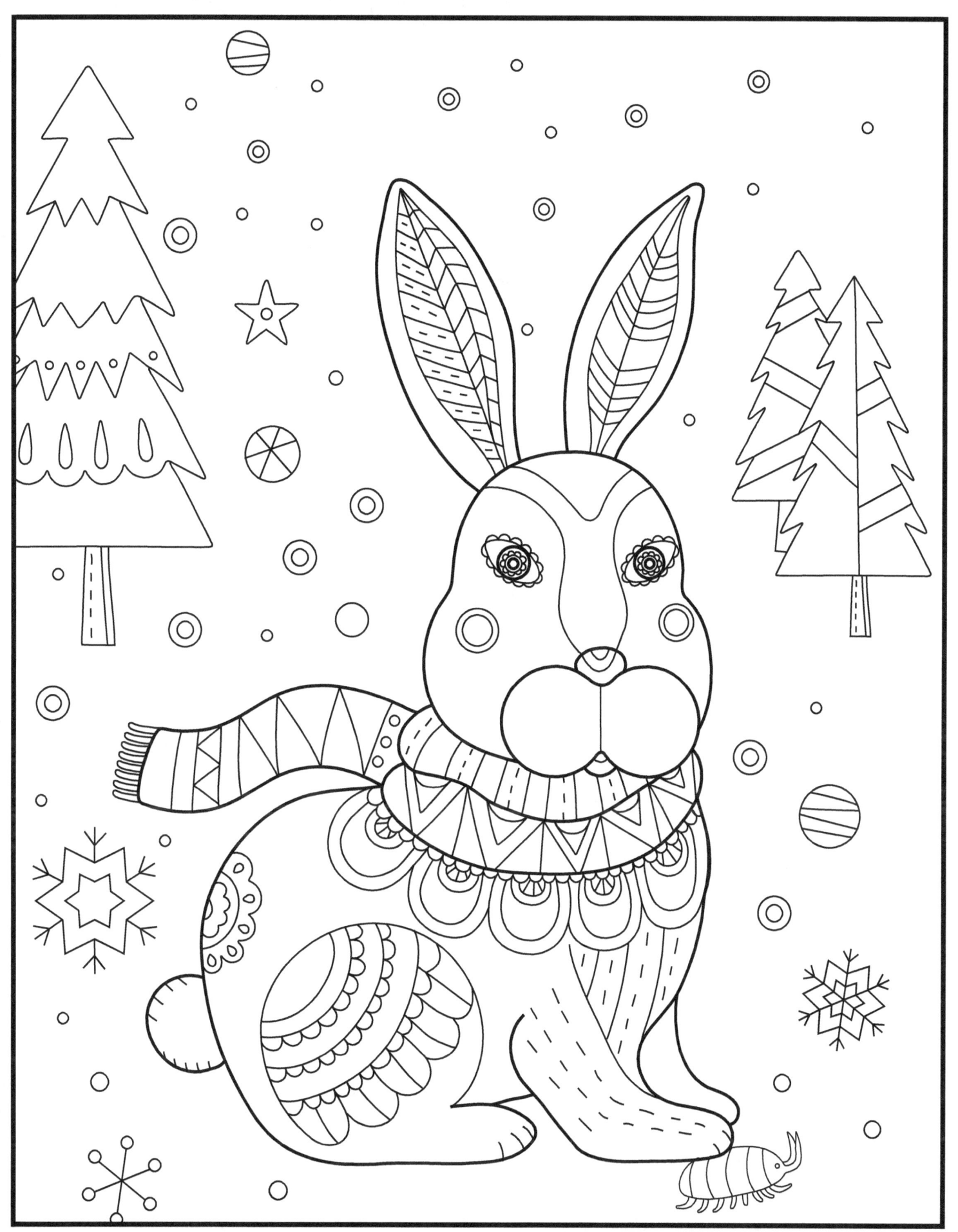

Mountain Hare (*Lepus timidus*).

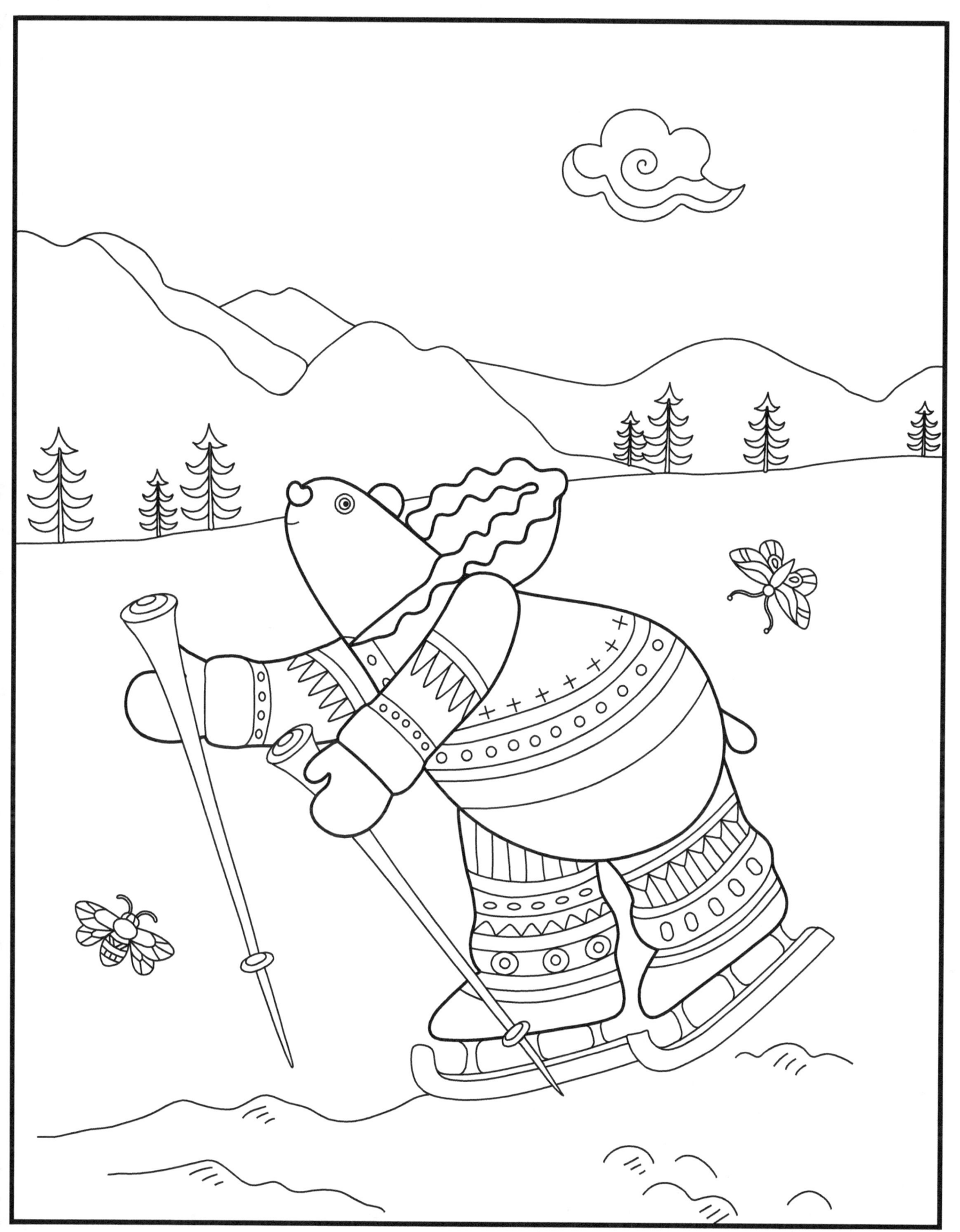

Polar Bear (*Ursus maritimus*).

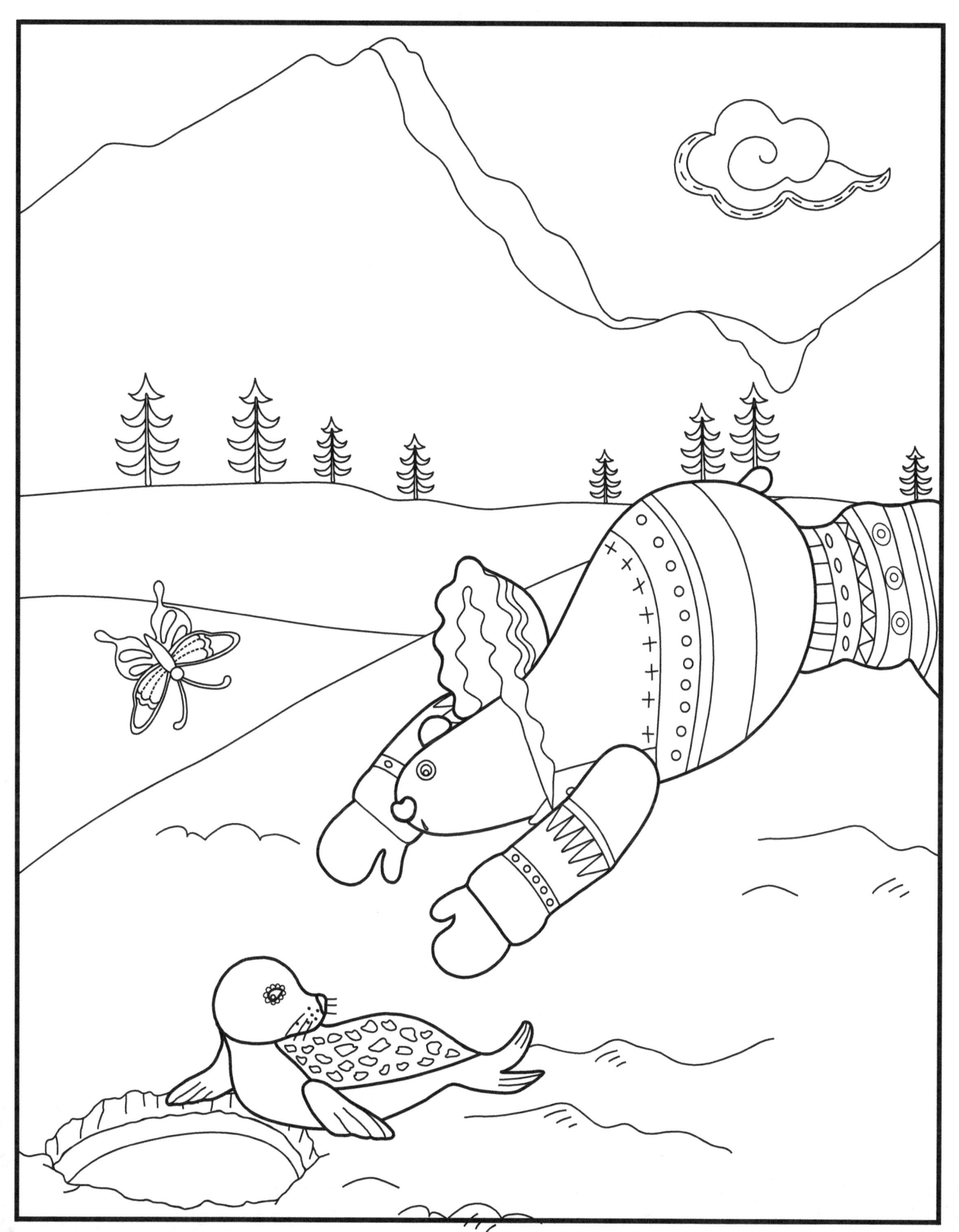

Polar Bear (*Ursus maritimus*).

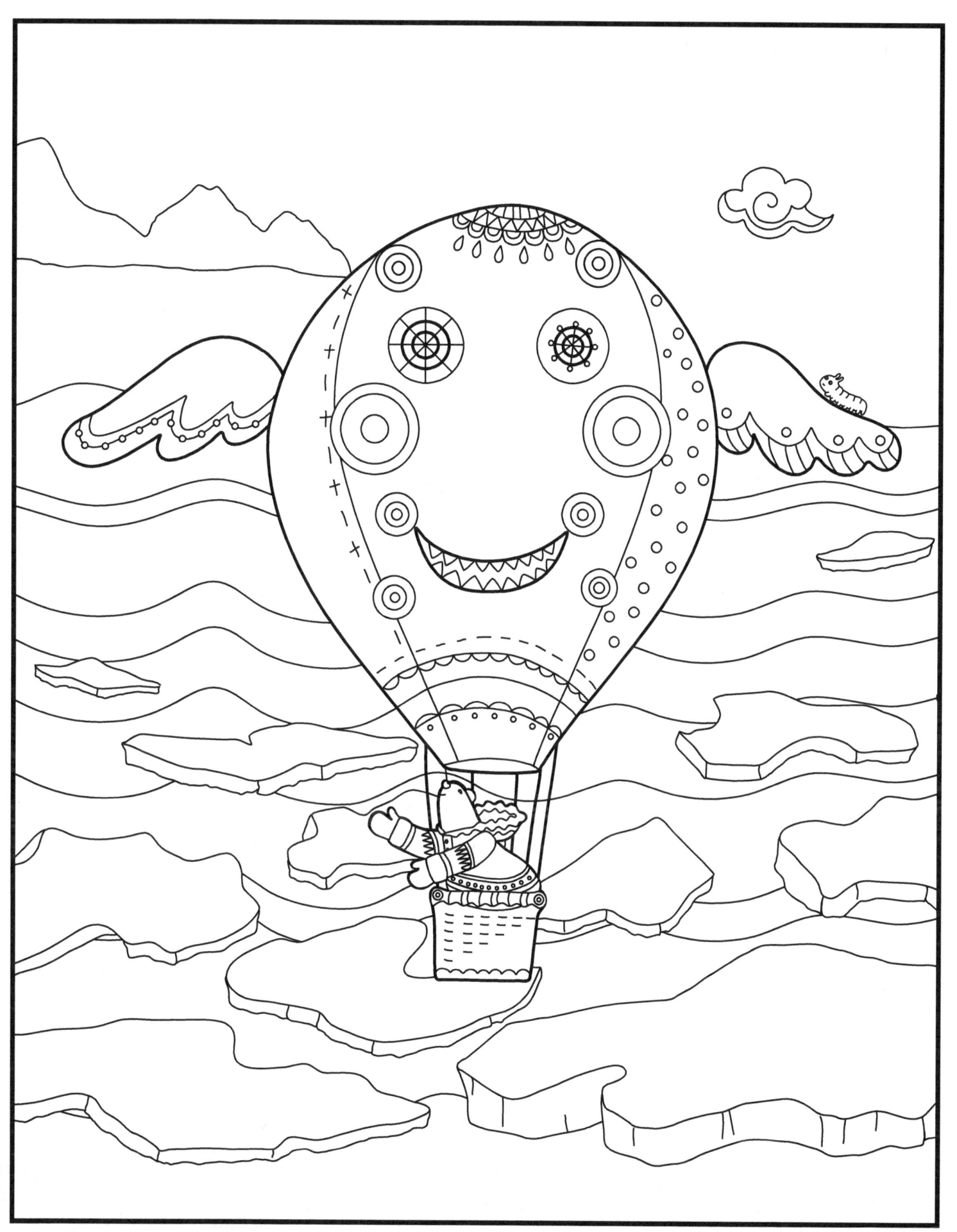

Polar Bear (*Ursus maritimus*).

Key to the Forest...

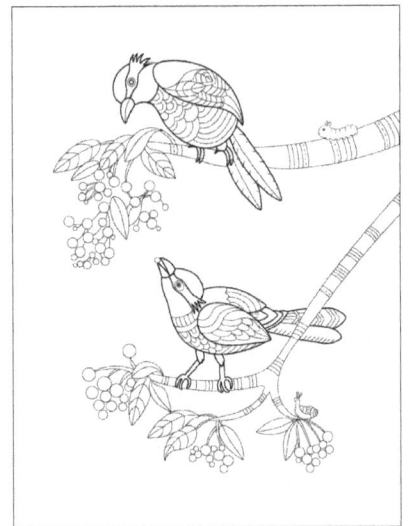

2 birds, 1 caterpillar, 1 snail

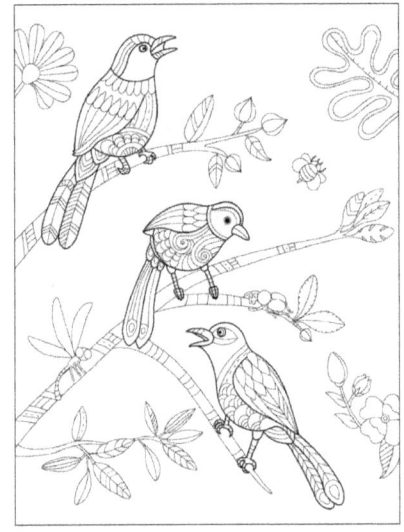

3 birds, 1 bee, 1 dragonfly, 1 beetle

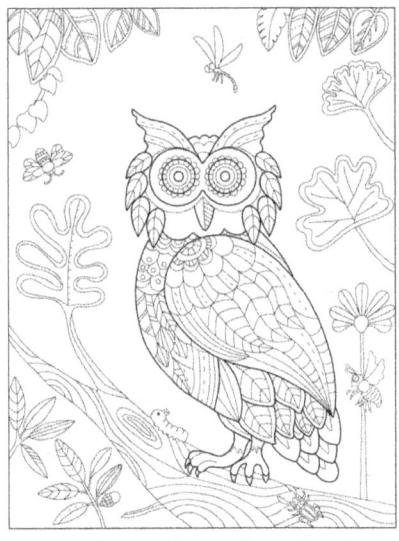

1 owl, 1 bee, 1 dragonfly, 2 beetles
1 caterpillar

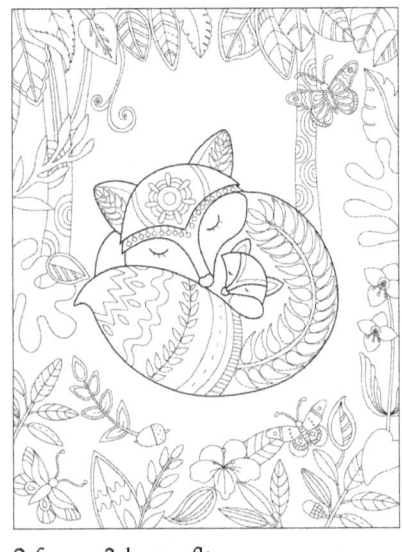

2 foxes, 3 butterflies

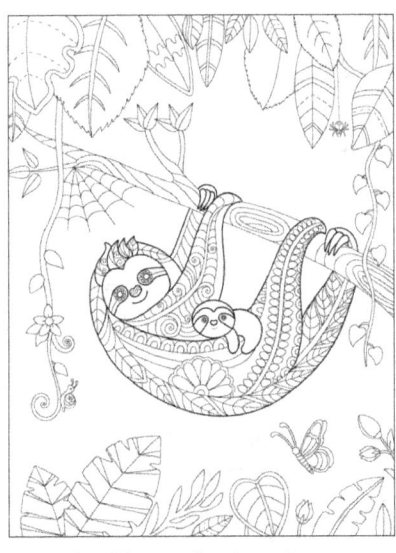

2 sloths, 1 butterfly, 1 spider

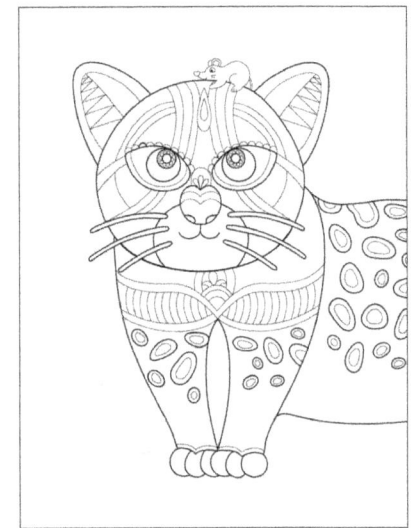

1 bobcat, 1 mouse

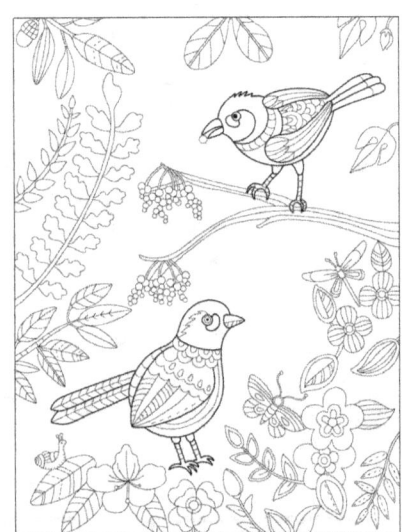

2 birds, 1 butterfly, 1 dragonfly,
1 snail

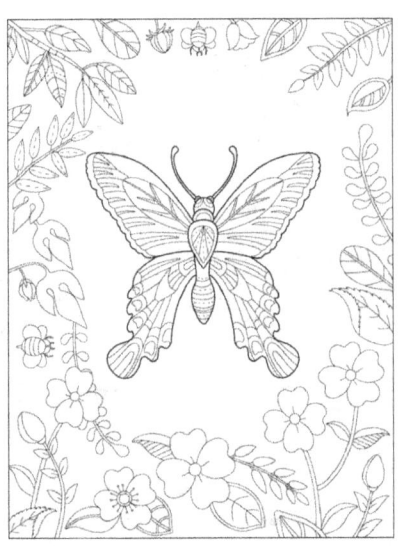

1 butterfly, 2 bees

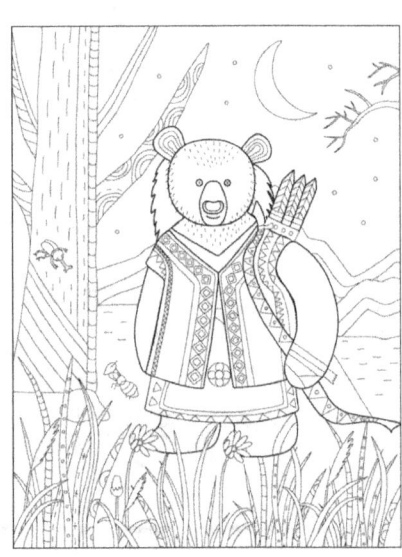

1 Asiatic black bear, 1 beetle, 1 ant

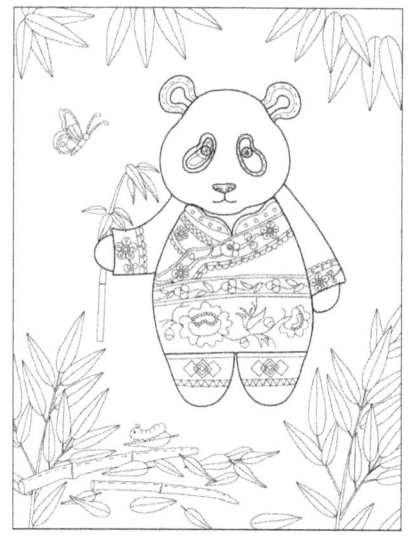

1 panda, 1 caterpillar, 1 butterfly

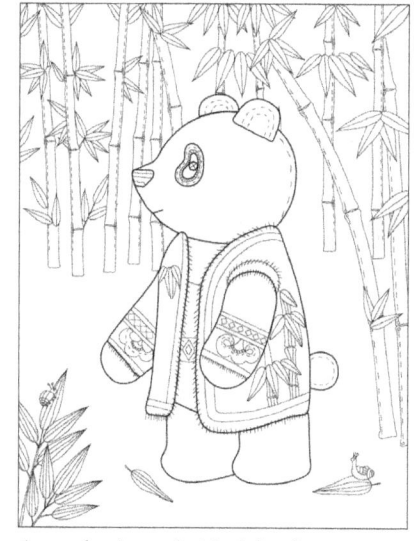

1 panda, 1 snail, 1 ladybird

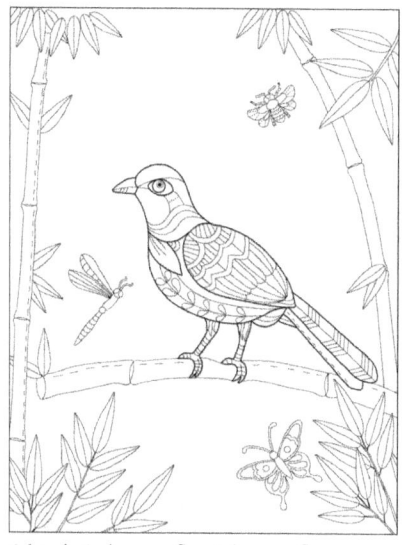

1 bird, 1 dragonfly, 1 butterfly
1 beetle

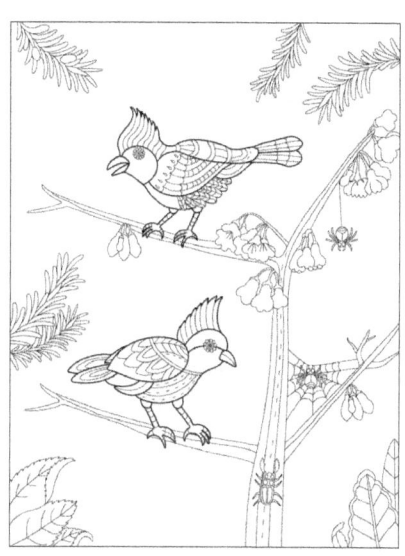

2 birds, 2 spiders, 1 beetle

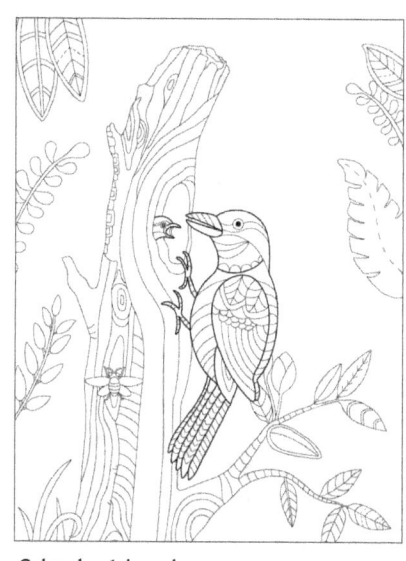

2 birds, 1 beetle

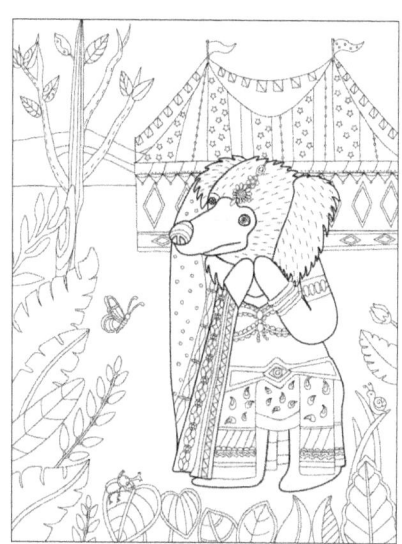

1 sloth bear, 1 butterfly, 1 snail
1 beetle

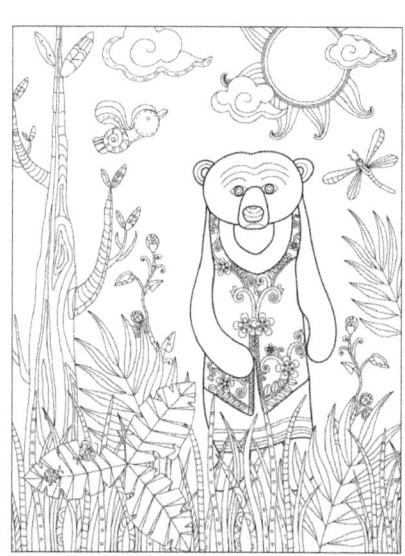

1 sun bear, 1 bird, 1 dragonfly,
2 ladybirds

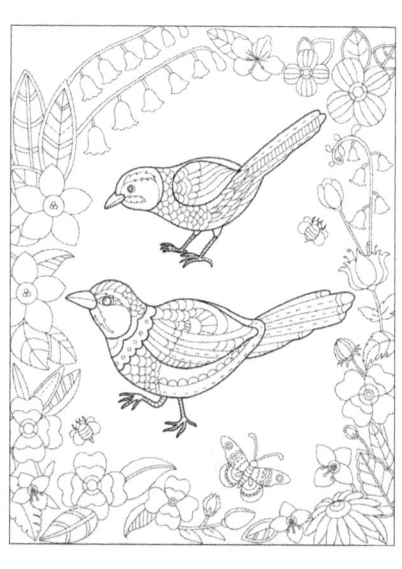

2 birds, 2 bees, 1 butterfly

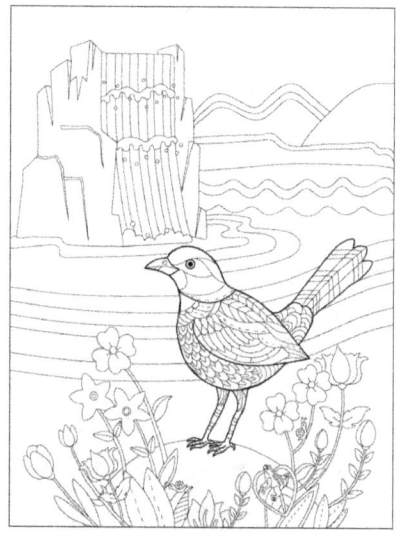

1 bird, 1 frog, 2 snails

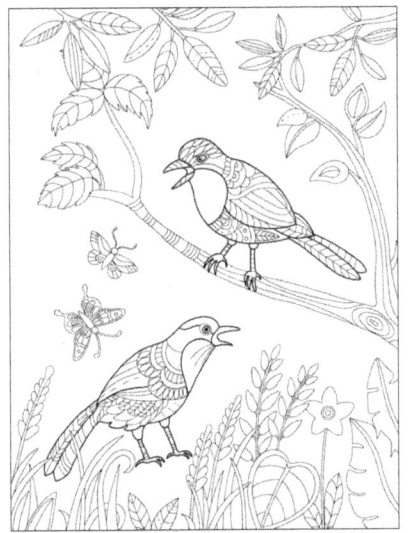

2 birds, 2 butterflies

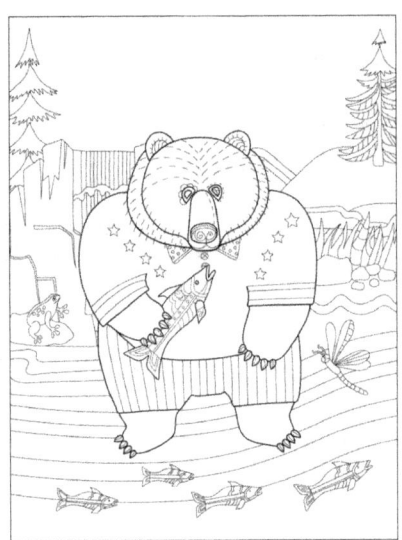

1 brown bear, 1 frog, 1 dragonfly
5 fish

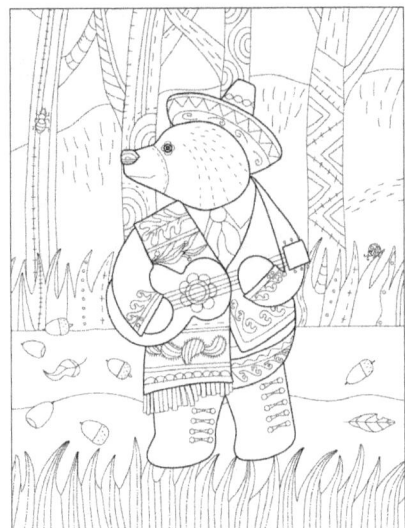

1 American black bear, 1 ladybird
1 ant

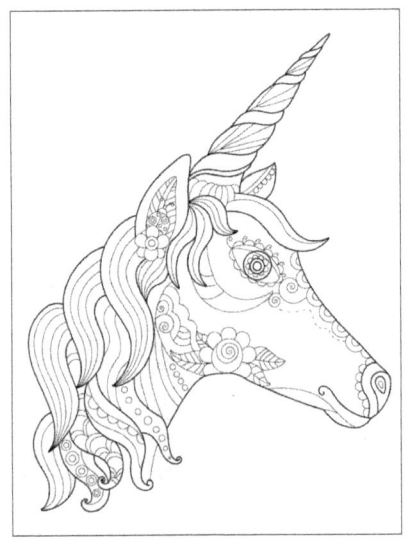

1 unicorn, 1 ladybird

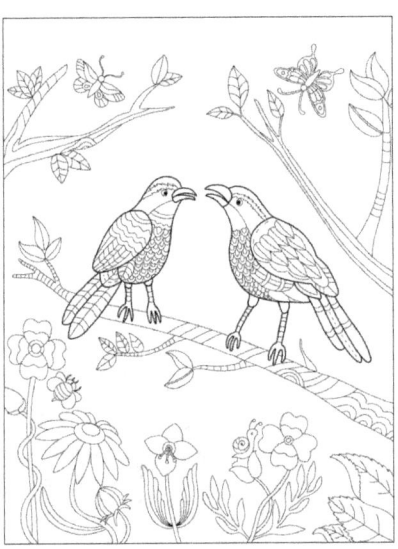

2 birds, 2 butterflies, 1 snail, 1 bee

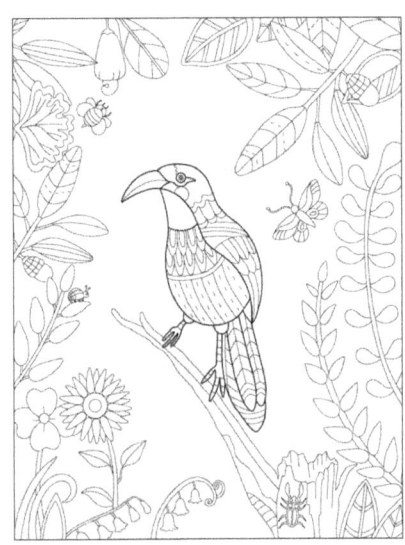

1 bird, 1 butterfly, 1 ladybird, 1 bee
1 beetle

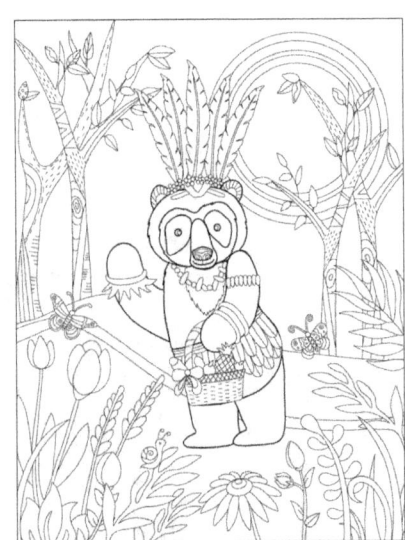

1 spectacled bear, 2 butterflies,
1 snail

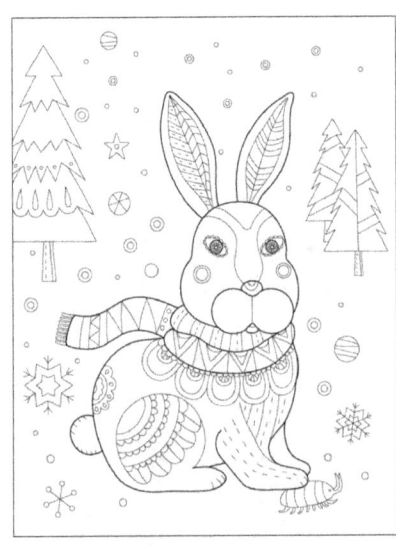

1 rabbit, 1 beetle

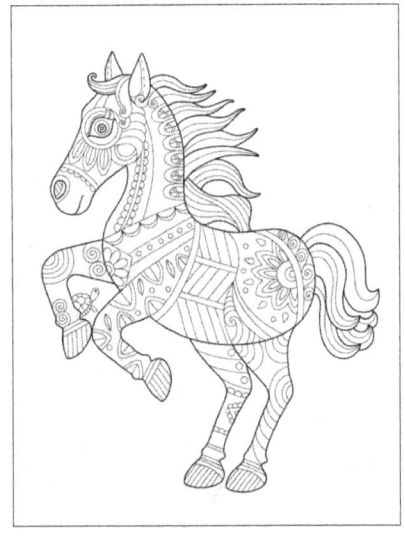

1 horse, 1 turtle

Key to the Polar Regions...

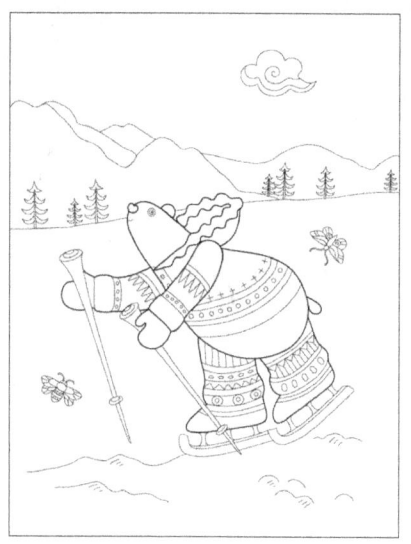

1 polar bear, 1 butterfly, 1 beetle

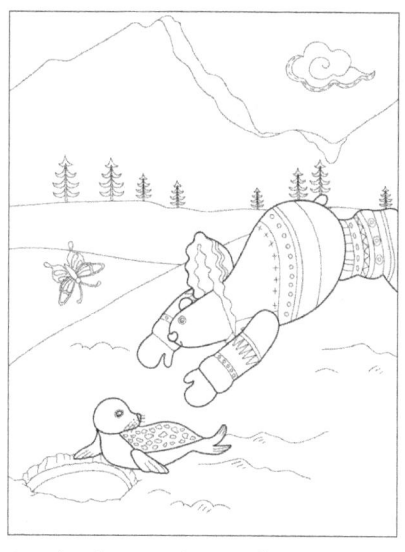

1 polar bear, 1 butterfly, 1 seal

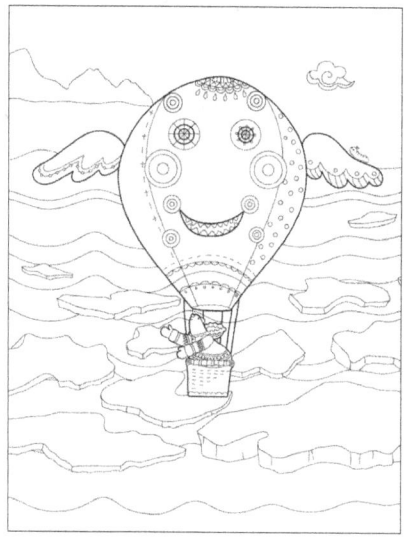

1 polar bear, 1 caterpillar

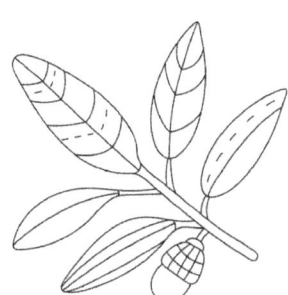

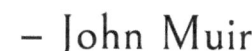

"And into the forest I go to lose my mind and find my soul"
– John Muir

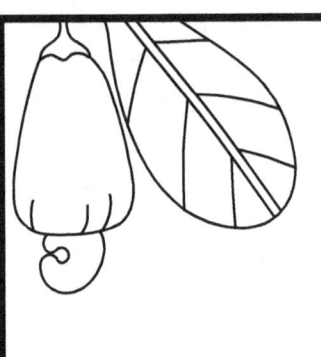

Color Palette Test Page

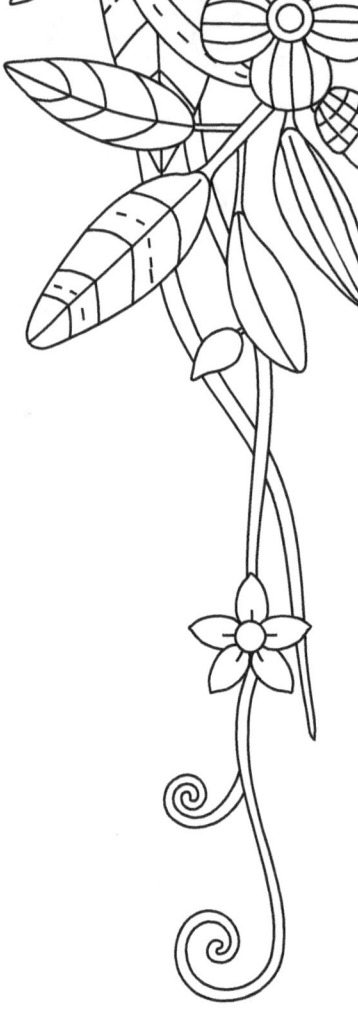

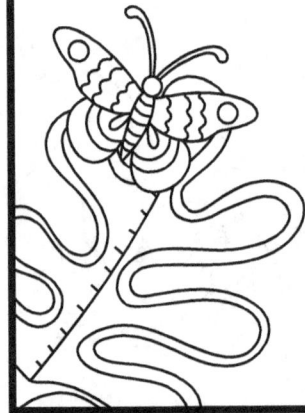

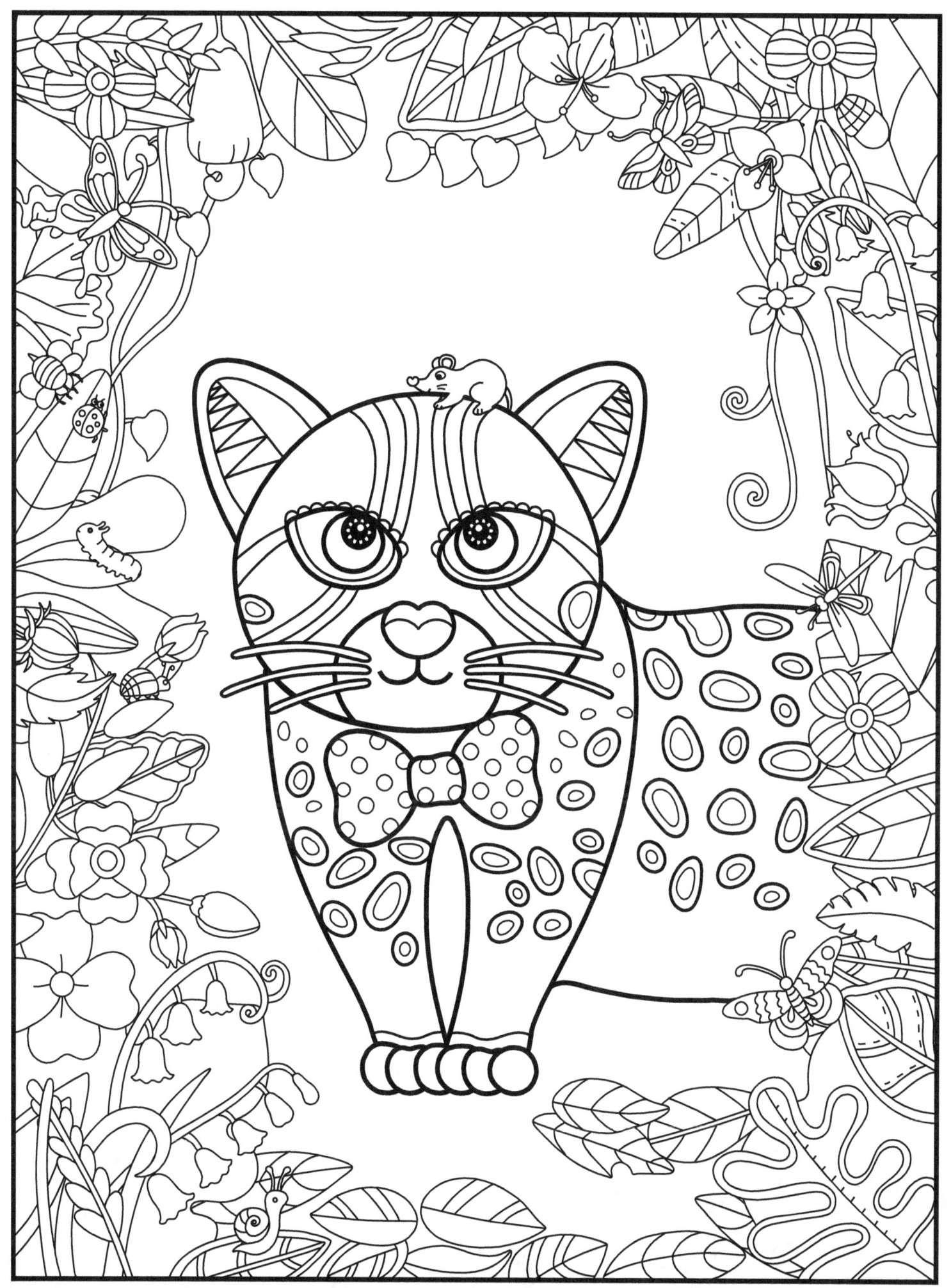

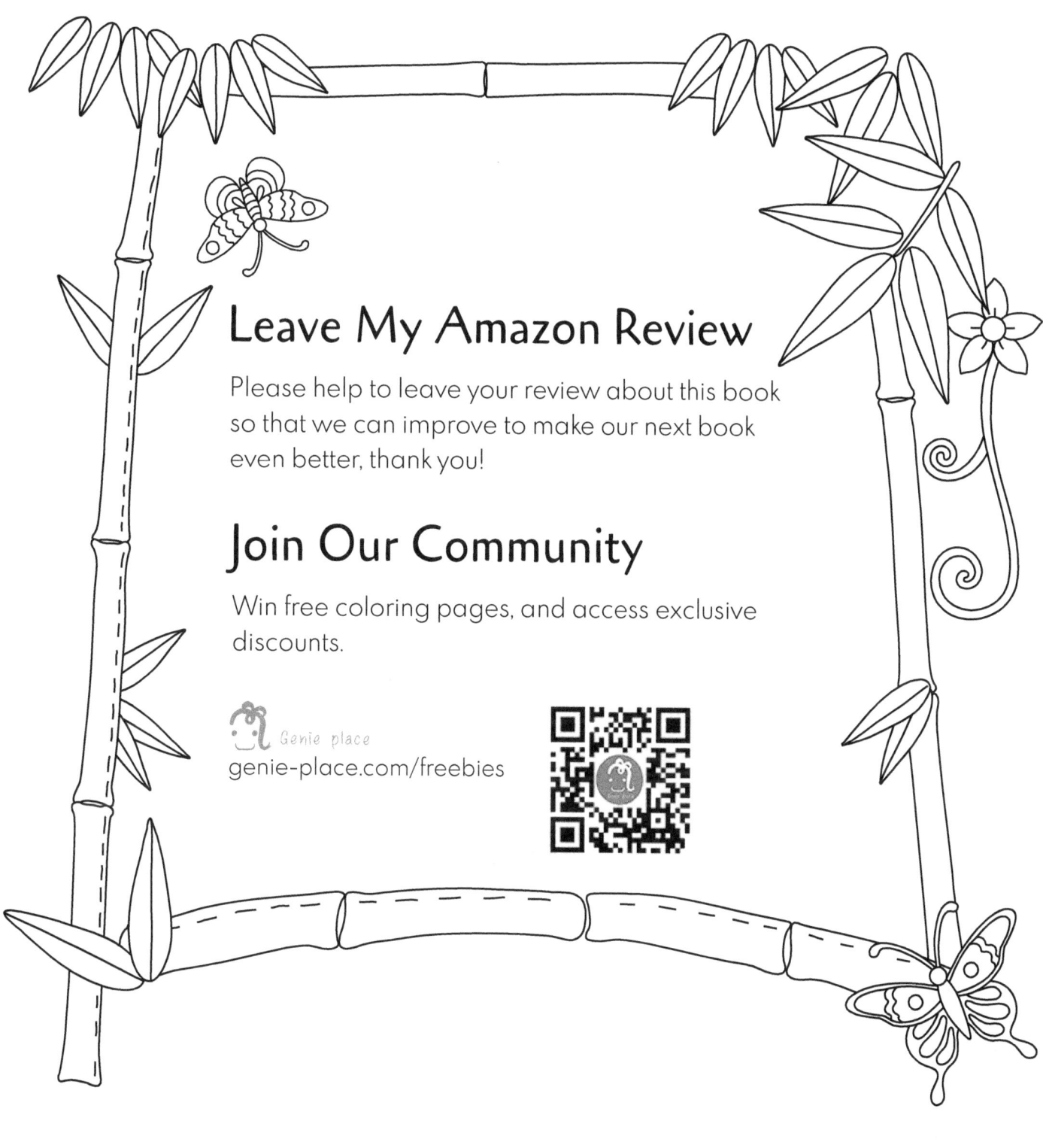

Leave My Amazon Review

Please help to leave your review about this book
so that we can improve to make our next book
even better, thank you!

Join Our Community

Win free coloring pages, and access exclusive
discounts.

Genie place
genie-place.com/freebies